FINDING MY FACE

The Memoir of a Puerto Rican American

Fernando Colón-López

Note for Librarians: a cataloguing record for this book that includes Dewey Decimal Classification and US Library of Congress numbers is available from the Library and Archives of Canada. The complete cataloguing record can be obtained from their online database at:
www.collectionscanada.ca/amicus/index-e.html
ISBN 1-4120-5307-2
Printed in Victoria, BC, Canada

Printed on paper with minimum 30% recycled fibre. Trafford's print shop runs on "green energy" from solar, wind and other environmentally-friendly power sources.

TRAFFORD

Offices in Canada, USA, Ireland and UK

This book was published *on-demand* in cooperation with Trafford Publishing. On-demand publishing is a unique process and service of making a book available for retail sale to the public taking advantage of on-demand manufacturing and Internet marketing. On-demand publishing includes promotions, retail sales, manufacturing, order fulfilment, accounting and collecting royalties on behalf of the author.

Book sales for North America and international:
Trafford Publishing, 6E–2333 Government St.,
Victoria, BC v8t 4p4 CANADA
phone 250 383 6864 (toll-free 1 888 232 4444)
fax 250 383 6804; email to orders@trafford.com
Book sales in Europe:
Trafford Publishing (uk) Ltd., Enterprise House, Wistaston Road Business Centre,
Wistaston Road, Crewe, Cheshire cw2 7rp UNITED KINGDOM
phone 01270 251 396 (local rate 0845 230 9601)
facsimile 01270 254 983; orders.uk@trafford.com
Order online at:
trafford.com/05-0202

10 9 8 7 6 5 4 3 2 1

~ TABLE OF CONTENTS ~

~ ACKNOWLEDGMENTS ~

This memoir would not have come to fruition without the love and support of my family and friends. My sincere and heartfelt thanks to the following:

Lois C. Colón my wife, for her steadfast unending love, patience and encouragement; our daughter, Kathleen Arrington for her unfailing support and the creativity she gave to the project; our sons Martin and Matthew for persevering with me through the vicissitudes of the journey.

My aunt and uncle Luz and Luis Villanueva, their daughter Nancy and her husband Moncho; my maternal second cousins Elisa, Eugenio, and Fernando López; and Carol and Arlene Bullock, my foster mother's grandchildren; Bill and Jean Carr my wife's sister and husband and my wife's other sister, Jan Wolgamont.

My friends Ava and Steve Gilzo, Bruce and Sara Gibb, Biff and Margie Barritt, Naomi Gottlieb, Doug Schoeninger, and Michael Lindvall. Special thanks to my friend Paul Stewart who was my unfailingly patient computer consultant, and to the many other family members and friends who supported and assisted me throughout this project.

Most especially I want to thank my loyal friend Monica McGoldrick whose unfailing persistence, patience and support enabled me to persevere until the memoir was published.

The cover photo is a view of my mother's family farm.

~ PROLOGUE ~

I am living what my father spoke of as a "better life". By my own definition it is, indeed, a wonderful life. I am married to a wonderful woman. We have three grown children. Each of them has brought more joy and meaning to my life than they will ever know. Each is married to someone who has expanded and deepened my life and added immeasurably to the love our family shares. We have three grandchildren who leave me speechless with the joy and wonder they bring. We are happily connected to our extended families. We have faithful friends and belong to a vital and committed church.

We have meaningful and rewarding work: I have been a practicing clinical psychologist for many years and my wife is a Presbyterian minister. We live in a community that offers endless opportunities for service and also an endless array of the best music, theater and film one could hope for. The university adds depth and challenge; the libraries are excellent. Bookstores abound. Our city is small and all this is right around the corner.

Our home has window walls overlooking fen and woodland where wildlife come, and we can watch birds come to the feeder all year long. The neighborhood offers walking and biking paths, and the river for canoeing and kayaking is a stone's throw away. When time allows we leave all this to travel and when we can arrange it we head for our cottage on the lake. There we can roam the beach and woods alone or gather for days of good times with family and friends.

It is indeed a wonderful life. It is not the way my life started.

My parents were born and raised in Puerto Rico. I was born and raised in the United States in foster homes. Because of the circumstances of my childhood it has taken me a while to know and to understand my Puerto Rican heritage and to put together a coherent sense of who I am.

In this memoir I tell the story of how I did this by successfully finding and reconnecting with my biological families in Puerto Rico. My family, friends and colleagues have encouraged me to write this memoir because they believe the story is important, as do I.

~ Beginnings ~

Margarita (Mother): 1905

I picture Margarita, my mother, as a little girl, brown eyes dancing and smiling shyly. I don't have a photo, but I do have stories: vivid stories that bring her into focus and enliven her imprint in my mind and heart. I never knew her, except from the womb, and yet her realness is always with me, and within the collective memory of her extended family as well.

She was born Margarita López-Massas on June 23, 1905. Her parents, Juan Ignacio López-Melendez and Juanita Massas-Reyes lived on a farm near Las Piedras, Puerto Rico. She was born on that farm, which was tucked in the rolling, intensely green hills nine miles from the eastern coast and about 13 miles from the southern coast. Geographically, it was paradise. I like to think the first year of her life was as exquisite as her surroundings.

When she was a year old her mother gave birth to twins: Dominga and Domingo. Both mother and son died in the birthing process, and Ignacio López was left alone with two daughters to raise: an infant and a one-year-old. Fortunately, the López-Massas families were closely knit, and various relatives who lived on adjoining farms cared for Margarita. Together they raised sugar, coffee, tobacco, fruits, vegetables and livestock. It was a rich environment for what must have been a grieving toddler.

The stories tell me that she enjoyed growing up in those hills, that caring and busy adults surrounded her, and that she had many cousins to play with. The generosities of her extended family encircled her. I know that made a big difference in her well-being. I like to think going to school until the 6th grade also helped. Some of the stories I've heard make me smile: that she was lovely, vivacious and energetic. I like to think her childhood smoothed out, because when she was thirteen her life was shattered again. Ignacio, her father, died of appendicitis, and so she and her sister Dominga were left parentless.

After her father's death, Margarita went to live with relatives, primarily with her Uncle Isaac López and his wife Elisa and their eight children. Although Margarita loved her aunt and uncle very much, and they loved her, her adolescent years were saturated with a deep sadness. She turned her attention to sewing, and became an excellent seamstress. She also learned to embroider, and then worked in a factory until she was 27. I'm not sure when she started there, but it gave her life a focus and made it possible for her to use her skills. She may have worked there 10 years.

But she was restless. She wanted a different opportunity.

Gregorio (Father): 1902

I picture Gregorio as a little boy, sturdy and square, with somber eyes and a smile that slowly crept across his face. Again, I don't have a photo but I do have the stories, and the stories of Gregorio are vivid too. They're crucial stories for me, helping me to try to understand the way my father's life unfolded. His realness is always with me too. Even though we never shared a home, the impact of his absence or his presence has been a defining factor in my life.

I don't know how much he smiled, this boy; but I hope it was more than I think it was. He was born Gregorio Colón-Torres on May 13, 1902. His parents, Domingo Angel Colón-Romero and Encarnacion Torres-Colón lived on a farm near Aibonito, Puerto Rico, which is in the foothills of the Central Cordillera, a ridge of mountains that runs along Puerto Rico's east-west axis. Aibonito translates "Oh Beautiful" and it IS that! 33 miles from the east coast and 14 miles from the south coast, its mountainous central location is breathtaking.

Gregorio was the fourth of 14 children, 10 who lived into adulthood: five boys and five girls. Life on the Aibonito farm was not easy. The cash crops there were eggs, fruits, coffee and tobacco, and they all required hard work. The children helped.

The stories about Gregorio's mother warm your heart. They are all told with immense gratitude. She was a warm, hard-working and caring woman, who nurtured her children and saw to their religious upbringing. Every Sunday she took them to church in Aibonito.

I like to think there were many stories of good times on that farm: among the children, maybe with the neighbors. Maybe trips into Aibonito were adventures and were enjoyed by the whole bunch. When I knew some of these aunts and uncles later, as adults, they absolutely knew how to celebrate! It was obvious they'd had some practice somewhere!

Some of the stories I heard from Gregorio himself: that he went to a rural one-room school until he completed the 5th grade, and that he was ashamed that his parents were too poor to buy him shoes. He went to school barefoot. The stories have it that he was quite intelligent. His teacher encouraged him, and tried to coax him into staying in school. But his father Domingo said no. Gregorio stopped school at age 10 to work on the farm.

Some of the stories make me cringe. Like this one: when Gregorio was about 13 his father sent him to town with eggs to sell to their customers. Gregorio sold the eggs, and then spent a few pennies to buy a sweet. When he got home and gave the money to his father, his father noticed the missing pennies. He asked what happened and Gregorio told him. Domingo beat Gregorio with a switch, then tied him to a crossbeam on the porch of the house where he left him for the rest of the day.

This is a harrowing story. He was eventually drenched in sweat and urine and in helplessness and fear and rage as well. When his father left the house in the evening to get a few drinks at a roadside stand, his distraught mother managed to cut him down and free him. It's hard to get your mind around such cruelty, and your heart seizes at the image.

I wonder what drove my grandfather to be so angry and harsh and cruel at times. I never found out. Once when I was talking with my father, when he was in his 70's, he acknowledged the truth of the story. He smiled, just a little, and said it was nothing to worry about. His father just believed he had to be very harsh with him. I couldn't stomach that, and I still can't. I think the cruelty Gregorio experienced at his father's hand fueled his desire to escape from the farm, which he did, at the age of 14. 1 think it also fueled his determination, which he had in spades all the rest of his life.

Gregorio ran away to his paternal grandfather's farm in Cayey, where he worked in a grocery store for four years. At 18 he returned home to Aibonito and worked on the farm once again, until he was 22. He also joined the National Guard of Puerto Rico.

GREGORIO: 1930

1930 brought a welcome change for Gregorio. While in the Guard he had carefully saved his money, and early in 1930 he immigrated to New York City. It was in the midst of the Great Depression. There were no jobs. Gregorio was forced to live from his savings for two years, catching menial jobs when he could, like shining shoes and washing dishes.

In 1934 Gregorio joined the U.S. Army. He was stationed in NY. Jamie López from Las Piedras, Puerto Rico was the only other Puerto Rican in the unit. They became friends. They horsed around together, and went to dances, and sometimes visited Jaimie's relatives who lived in the city.

MARGARITA: 1932

The autumn of 1932 brought a welcome change for Margarita, too. She left the factory. With the help of one of her Uncle Isaac's sons, her cousin Jaimie López, she immigrated to NYC where she lived for two years with distant relatives from Puerto Rico, Quelin and Lele Falero. The Falero's were enterprising and fun, and Margarita embraced her new life with enthusiasm. She saw her cousin Jaimie often. The stories have it that he kept a close watch over her.

When she'd been in NYC for about a year and a half, Jaimie introduced her to his friend Gregorio Colón. It wasn't the first time she'd seen Gregorio. They had both attended a baptism at the Baptist Church and a dance in Spanish Harlem. They had their eyes on each other.

On December 20, 1934 Margarita and Gregorio were married at the First Baptist Church in Spanish Harlem in NYC. Their reception was held at the Falero's apartment. The Falero's were there, and I know Jaimie was there. I wonder who else attended.

~ I Was Born ~
ON SEPTEMBER 19, 1935

FERNANDO: 1935

At my birth, tragedy came to Margarita's life once again, and to my life as well. My mother suffered a severe post-partum depression, and remained hospitalized in Beth David Hospital in Manhattan for six weeks. My mother was 30 when I was born; my father was 33.

When I was 27 days old my father admitted me to the Edwin Gould Foundation for Children, run by the Manhattan Department of Public Welfare, because my mother couldn't care for me, and neither could he. This was a holding institution, like an orphanage, that kept children until they could be placed in foster or adoptive care.

As an adult, and as a part of my search for my history, I succeeded in obtaining a copy of my file from that orphanage. In the file was a description of my father, and it brought him into focus for me. He was described as "being of medium height, rather good looking, with fine features, somewhat dark skin, dark eyes and black hair. He is immaculately clean in person and dress. He seems somewhat reticent in giving personal information." The case worker went on to surmise that because of his courteous behavior in the interview "he is a member of a rather high family, but is the one who failed to adjust to the home situation and came to the U.S. to seek his fortune."

After being in the orphanage for six weeks, I was placed in my first foster home on November 6, 1935. My foster mother was Mrs. K, who lived in Queens Village on Long Island, NY. My father later described Mrs. K as being a "very nice German lady" who was an excellent foster mother and in whose care I flourished. When he visited me he found me to be a happy, smiling baby. I will be forever grateful to Mrs. K.

Mrs. K was a nurse, and when her elderly mother became ill she needed to care for her. The case notes reported that "with tears in her eyes" she returned me to the Sheltering Arms Children's Service in NYC, the foster care agency which chose and supervised my foster home placements.

After my five-month placement with Mrs. K, I was placed in Mrs. M's foster home on March 27, 1936. She lived in the Bronx, and was of German origin. She was married to an Italian man. They had a 14-year-old son.

FERNANDO: 1936-1937

My time with the M's turned out to be disastrous. After I was placed with them, my father left the area for duty with the army. He visited me again when he was on furlough. I was two years old. He reports being shocked to see that I was in a filthy diaper and covered with flies. He said he saw that I had become quiet and withdrawn, and that the foster family seemed to enjoy yelling at me.

He reported the situation at once, and I was transferred the next day, on November 11, 1937, to my third foster home. My third foster mother and father were Emma Hauck and Harry Stewart. They lived in Elmont, NY, on Long Island. Mom Hauck was a Swiss-German immigrant, and Dad Stewart's heritage was English. This was a loving and caring home, and I had reached my last foster placement. I remained there until I graduated from high school and left for college, just before I was 18.

FOSTER MOTHER EMMA HAUCK: 1936

When Emma Hauck applied to the Sheltering Arms Children's Service to become

a foster parent she was 44 years old and Harry Stewart was 54. Emma was born in Bern, Switzerland. Her father, Rudolph Berman, was a brewmaster. Emma was the fifth of nine children, seven of whom survived. Four of her siblings remained in Switzerland, and two came to the U.S. One was a sister, Elizabeth, whose husband ran a delicatessen in California. They weren't able to see each other much, living on opposite coasts as they did. A brother, Frederick, lived in Cleveland, Ohio.

Mom Hauck described her childhood as having been very strict and very happy. In the midst of this strict environment she said the children were never "whipped," but none of them would have dared to say "no" to either of their parents. Mom told the caseworker that she had finished seventh grade at the age of 14, and then went to work. Her first job was learning how to be a cook. Later she went to France to hire out as a laundress to a countess because she wanted to learn French. When she returned to Switzerland she was a waitress in a hotel. She was no stranger to hard work. When Emma began to work she gave all her wages to her mother, who always put half of the amount in a savings account in Emma's name. After immigrating to the U.S. and finding work, Mom reported telling her mother to spend the money because she didn't need it. That was Emma.

It was a friend of Emma's who convinced her to immigrate to the U.S. She persuaded Emma that more money could be made in the States than in Europe, and so Emma took the chance. She located in Brooklyn, but was unable to get a job because she couldn't speak English. Finally, she took a job as a nursemaid for three children in a baker's family. It was there that she became acquainted with her future husband, George Hauck, who was a regular customer at the bakery. The story has it that he was smitten by this slender, very attractive blue-eyed blond with the radiant smile. George implored his mother to teach him a few words of German. When he spoke these words to Emma she was delighted. She knew no one who spoke German and was often very lonely.

After a year's acquaintance Emma and George were married on April 2, 1911 at the Graham Avenue Reformed Church in Brooklyn. Mom Hauck described her husband as a small, quiet man, who never liked to invite friends to their home. He didn't like to go out with the family, either, though he was always ready to give the family money to go out themselves. He spent most of his evenings at a pinochle club, or at his brother-in-law's saloon, and frequently kept late hours. He was born in Brooklyn of German parents. He completed the seventh grade and then became a glassblower. One firm regularly employed him for 20 years, which meant a lot to the family. He died when he was 45 from pneumonia. He and Emma had been married 15 years.

Emma and George had one child, Madeline, and her upbringing was strict as well. Mom told me George never "whipped" Madeline, but he was short with her, and never allowed her to talk at meals. The story has it that he paid little attention to her and never really knew her very well. Madeline spoke German until she was three years old. When she learned English from the neighbors she refused to speak German at all, always answering her mother in English. So when Madeline began school, Mom would study her schoolbooks in order to learn English herself, and she did. Madeline finished the eighth grade and went on to high school. She wasn't a conscientious student, so Mom decided that she might as well go to work as to "fool around in school". Mom found Madeline a job as a cashier in a butcher shop, and then when she was 15 she was trained as a telephone operator. She worked as an operator until she was married to Alexander Bullock on September 16, 1934 when she was 33 years old. I was always grateful to have Madeline in my life. She was like a friendly aunt. Her children, Carol, Arlene, and Wesley were my contemporaries and they were an integral part of my family life.

FOSTER FATHER HARRY STEWART: 1936

Prior to George Hauck's death, Harry Stewart, who was a distant cousin of George's, became a boarder in the Hauck household. When George died, the family (which now consisted of Emma, 14 year old Madeline and Harry Stewart) moved to a house on "M" Street in Elmont, on Long Island, which Harry and Emma had built themselves.

Harry was 10 years older than Emma. He had been a taxi driver in Brooklyn, and he continued to drive a taxi in Elmont. He'd also been a licensed tugboat pilot and had worked in New York harbor. He was interested in politics and was the secretary for his ward.

Harry helped Emma get house cleaning jobs with the teachers who rode his taxi. They were able to make ends meet. Mom told me she felt that Harry had been a better father to Madeline than her own father, George, had been. He liked to play with her and gave her toys.

He was married at one time, and described his wife as a "church worker" and an organist. She lived in California. Their only child, a girl, died, and his wife never wanted another child. They were married 25 years before they separated.

EMMA HAUCK AND HARRY STEWART, FOSTER PARENTS: 1936-1954

I find it interesting that the Sheltering Arms Children's Service made its three home visits to Emma Hauck's, to assess her home for possible foster care, on September 7, 11 and 12, 1934, just before Madeline's wedding to Al Bullock on September 16. I don't think Emma and Harry wanted an empty house. Madeline and Al had three children: Carol, Arlene and Wesley who were like half siblings to me. Carol was the oldest and about my age.

As part of my search for my own childhood I was able to get the case notes from the Sheltering Arms Agency. Those notes were descriptive. The caseworker gathered that "Mrs. Hauck's marriage to George Hauck had not been particularly happy because George was away from home a lot and took little interest in his family. However, Mrs. Hauck's affection for her daughter, her relations with her friends, her interest in caring for her home and her ability to help support the family financially point to adequate interest and satisfaction. Mrs. Hauck does not impress one at all as a person who considers her life to have been an unhappy one. On the contrary, she is particularly serene and cheerful. She has had several domestic jobs since her husband's death and she has boarded children privately. The two year old child from next door spends much of her time at Mrs. Hauck's, where she gets better care than at home. Mrs. Hauck frequently makes clothes for neighbor's children who need them, or takes care of a neighbor's cat or dog during the neighbor's absence. One gets the impression that her chief satisfactions come from caring for a child or an animal who seem to need her. At the end of the evaluation, Mrs. Hauck expressed the wish that all agencies investigate equally carefully, as she believed that children are often improperly placed." I could tell that this was seen as being typical of her interest in children.

The caseworker was also impressed by Emma Hauck's frugality: she had $4,033 in one savings account, $2,000 in another, and owned the house that she and Harry built.

Mom Hauck

Mom also had a close circle of women friends who spoke German. These women got together on a regular basis to sew, gossip, laugh, eat sweets and support each other. Two of the women were also foster mothers and served as references when she applied for foster mother status herself.

FERNANDO WITH EMMA AND HARRY: 1937-1951

My earliest memory is of arriving in this home, being very quiet, saying nothing for a number of months even though I was able to talk. I was terrified, and didn't know what would happen. Mom and Dad kept coaxing me to talk. Mom fed me whenever she could because she worried about me being so skinny. They fussed over me and encouraged me. I began to thaw.

My father visited me after the customary 6-month wait. All was not rosy. Mom Hauck was "despairing" because I was such a "nervous child, and wouldn't talk or bathe". She wondered if she should keep me. But she did, and finally I felt safe enough to talk and to participate in family life. Even so, I also remember rocking myself to sleep for several years after, to comfort myself, I suppose, as I learned to live in what turned out to be an amazing place.

When I arrived at Mom and Dad's house there were five other foster children there. Three of them were siblings Angela, Felix and Sarah Rodriquez, and they were Puerto Rican! They were just a little older than I was, and they eventually returned to their family. Next came Alvin Lenox and Stanley Berghauser. Then a series of seven more foster brothers replaced them; these boys stayed for varying lengths of time. I must mention their names: Johnnie West, Ralph Weider, Walter Reinhardt, Kenneth Dorsey, Ted McGrath, John Williams and Dennis Ilgin. Their names are significant, not only because they identify these brave boys, but also because their names point to their heritage. None were Puerto Rican. I was the only dark complexioned one in my family after Angela and Felix and Sarah left. That fact did not escape my attention.

Another early memory is of Mom's insistence that we attend Sunday School and church each Sunday. That insistence turned out to be one of the great gifts she gave me. When I was three, she walked me to the churchyard and pointed to a door. She told me to go through the door and Mrs. Smith would be on the other side to greet me. The astounding thing to me is that, shy as I was, I did it. Mrs. Smith turned out to be a warm and wonderful woman, and so began my religious education.

This church was the Community Presbyterian Church in Elmont. It was in a working class neighborhood, and the experience there was rich. I took it all in. I enjoyed Sunday School when I was young, and as I grew I couldn't wait to get to church on Sunday to hear our pastor preach. It was odd, because I remember him as a rather grouchy old bachelor who smoked smelly cigars and had little ability to relate to children. But his preaching I found compelling, even as an adolescent. He opened my mind and heart to the treasures of Christian theology, and to art, literature and music. Being a member of that church was a powerful, enriching and profound experience.

My school experience was rich, too, and very positive. Mrs. Hotchkiss was my first grade teacher, and she was wonderful. She made learning fun. She gave us individual attention and encouraged us to do our best. She was "fluffy" too, and wore a wonderful perfume. Here's to Mrs. Hotchkiss, wherever she may be!

Grades 2-5 were positive also. I was a good student and I loved to learn. I got a lot of affirmation for my scholastic ability. It culminated in the 6th grade when I was honored, along with two other students, as one of the top students in the class. There was a celebration: dinner and games, and gifts for the three of us in recognition of our academic achievement. At the 6th grade graduation ceremony I was selected to give a "commencement" speech.

My topic was Benjamin Franklin. My 6th grade teacher, Mrs. Lillian Cobb, coached me through the process of choosing the reference books on Franklin, taking notes (she then discussed the notes with me) and constructing the speech. She encouraged me not to read the speech but to memorize it, which I did. I remember that graduation well.

In the midst of it all, my foster brothers came and went. They stayed for varying pieces of time. Sometimes I was the youngest child. Sometimes I was the oldest. My sibling position within the family shifted many times. My foster brothers left for a variety of reasons: some returned to their families, one was adopted, two went to an institution for the mentally and emotionally retarded. Two more went to reform school and others went on to still another foster home.

Amidst all the comings and goings, life at 11 "M" Street in Elmont was bustling and busy. As I mentioned before, Mom and Dad had built this "M" Street house, on an 80' by 100' lot. There are many wonderful stories about the process, because they were challenged by Dad's lingering disability from childhood polio. He had a stiff hip and a short leg, and this meant he couldn't get up on the roof. So Mom did all the shingling, and she did it well, too. The loss of some of her fingernails as she hammered became insignificant in light of the overall accomplishment! This hometown of Elmont was an unincorporated town on Long Island, in Nassau County. We lived in a neighborhood of modest homes owned by blue-collar families. On one side of us lived a very taciturn Irish family. But on the other side of us was an Italian family, on a double lot, with a house and large flower and vegetable gardens. On weekends their extended families came from NYC for wonderful, noisy feasts complete with music, arguments and laughter. I felt drawn to the color and earthiness of those good people, darker skinned, a bit like me.

The rest of the neighborhood was Irish and Italian, too, with a lot of German families as well. We all played throughout the neighborhood: baseball in the street, basketball with the basket hoop on the telephone pole and always, catch with the kids next door.

Mom Hauck and Dad Stewart turned out to be truly wonderful foster parents. Initially, their home was on an unpaved street in the country with empty wooded lots around. Nearby were open fields, used by farmers to raise

vegetables which they trucked to the city to sell. Mom grew a vegetable and a flower garden, and raised a hundred new chicks every year. Those chickens lived in a coop, and in a fenced-in area on an empty lot behind our house. The chicken manure was used to fertilize the garden, and eventually formed rich soil a foot deep. You could grow anything in that soil! Mom canned tomatoes, and made ketchup and wine (there was a grape arbor too). She preserved sauerkraut, jelly, jam and eggs. We had a cold cellar where we buried turnips and potatoes for use in the winter. I remember bunches of onions hanging to dry in a small outbuilding. Mom used it all: she was an excellent cook and baker, and the food flowed. She loved to feed us all. There was abundance.

I have very fond memories of Mom and Dad's house. It was a modest but well kept home, located in a blue-collar neighborhood. There was a sun/sitting room in front, a dining room, three bedrooms, a kitchen, a back room and a bath. There was also a basement. We had our meals in the kitchen on a table that overlooked our flower and vegetable gardens. The kitchen had a combination gas/coal stove upon which Mom cooked her excellent meals. The kitchen was the heart of the home, especially when it was cold and we gathered there to be near the warmth of the stove and to play cards and other games and to do our homework. After wonderful meals we boys would take turns doing the dishes. Each of us also had house chores, which we did on a regular basis. Everyone had to do their part, both inside the house and outside in the yard.

Dad Stewart was very capable too. He was able to fix, repair and maintain anything in the house that needed attention. Part of the garage was used for his tools and his workbench. He'd constantly put different sized bikes together for us kids as we continually grew. At Eastertime he would paint eggs and then gave them as gifts to friends and neighbors. I also recall his avid interest in politics: he read the paper and listened to the radio news every day. He also liked to play cards, and he taught us to play too. There was many a Saturday night spent around the kitchen table playing pinochle. Another cherished memory is the set of Lincoln Logs he made for me. He made one piece each day and gave it to me when I came home from school. Finally, I had a whole set.

One could not hope for a better foster home situation.

In the photos that follow, the first is of Dad Stewart with seven children and Mom reaching out to comfort me. This picture was taken when I was 2 or 3 years old. The tallest boy, the boy next to me, is Alvin. On the far left is Stanley. Angela is next to him. Felix is next to Dad and Sarah is next to Felix. (Angela, Felix and Sarah were the siblings.) Carol, Mom's granddaughter, is the blond girl in front. Six foster children and Mom's grandchild: quite a household!

The second photo is of Alvin, me and Stanley when I'm about 5 years old. I'm wearing my birthday-gift cowboy outfit.

Without question I was very fortunate to have landed in a very wholesome and solid foster family situation. Even so, I had a number of experiences while I was growing up that unsettled me.

The most profound one occurred when I was about seven years old. Since my father had visited me occasionally while on leave from the army, these visits naturally led me to wonder about my mother. I wondered what had happened to her and where she was. I asked Mom Hauck and Dad Stewart about my mother, but they had no answers. Maybe it was because of my questions, maybe it was in response to my foster parents' urging, or maybe there was advice to my father from my caseworker: something must have precipitated my father's visit to tell me about my mother when I was seven years old. I still remember vividly that particular visit. After talking a while with me, Mom Hauck and Dad Stewart my father suggested to me that the two of us take a walk around the block. During the walk I imagine he said something like, "I understand you've been asking questions about your mother and you want to know what happened to her." I certainly must have said "Yes", and then he said, "Fernando, after you were born your mother got sick with a fever and had to stay in the hospital. She didn't get better and she eventually died. We had hoped to have a lot of children, but of course we couldn't when she died. And that's why I had to give you to Emma Hauck, so she could raise you. I'm still in the army."

I was shocked, stunned and saddened by this story about my mother. I was just quiet after he told me, and as I remember thinking about it I remember realizing that I would never get to see her. I must have buried the knowledge of her death very quickly, although I do remember being very upset about it. I may have talked more about it with my father and my foster parents, but I don't remember doing so. It was the saddest day of my life: now I knew for sure that she was gone forever.

While I was growing up I did get to see some members of my biological family. I remember from my elementary years visits from people who came to "M" Street, just to see me. One visit was from my fathers sister, Berta, and her husband Tony, and their daughter Iris, who was my age. I was intrigued by the visit and I enjoyed spending the whole day with them. They were very warm and outgoing, and they were darker-skinned, like me. I wasn't able to see my father much, and this visit was an important-for-me connection with my biological family.

When I was about 11 years old another group of darker-skinned people visited me. Their skin color always intrigued me, because I had no other contact with people who looked like me. This group consisted of my father, an army friend of his, an older man and a young boy my age. We had a good time, but it was strange, because my father didn't tell me who all these people were. Before they left, the older man took a picture of me with my pet dog, Butch.

The most difficult recurring experience that I had was that of having twelve foster siblings come and go during the fifteen years that I lived with Mom Hauck. Each time a new foster brother arrived it was exciting. The curiosity about what this boy would be like always carried the day. However, when each of them eventually left it was another story. It was devastating, repeatedly devastating, because besides the grief of losing that particular boy it confronted me again and again with the fact that I, too, one day could be taken and sent away. When I was a preschooler I coped with this reality as best I could. When I was in elementary school I would get very tense and anxious about these departures, and I recall long times when my stomach would be knotted with tension and I would become constipated. I was terrified, and the terror manifested itself viscerally. When I was older and in my teens, I would continue to "freak out" at these junctures, but I coped by becoming quiet and depressed. It wasn't until I went to graduate school, and then became a clinical psychologist, that I finally put all the pieces together about the arrivals and the departures, and what an impact they had upon my life. Never again was I to see any of these foster brothers after they left our home. It was as if each one of them had died and I was left to grieve and mourn each one of them. These were very sad, depressing and difficult times for me.

One way I coped with the underlying tension and fear of departure that at times pervaded the house was to escape to a tree house I had built on an empty wooded lot near our home. I'd spend many hours, and many days even, in the peace and solitude of that marvelous tree house. - It was my safe haven. It was 20 feet off the ground and sometimes it would sway gently in the wind. I would listen to the birds singing and the squirrels chattering and watch the sunlight playing through the green leaves of the oak tree. When I was in my early teens a hurricane blew through Long Island. It tore down utility lines, smashed houses and uprooted trees. My oak tree with my tree house in it stood.

Another way I coped with these tensions was by focusing my energy on school, sports and household chores. Fortunately, I remained a good student, and continued to love to learn. Mom totally supported my academic endeavors, always demanding that I do my homework before my chores. I was good at sports, which was lucky for me, and I had fun being on teams. I had an especially good friend in high school, Larry Rauchut. Larry was this great extroverted, fun loving guy. We had some classes together, and began hanging out. He had an old car, a 1934 Ford coupe, dark blue with black fenders and yellow wire wheels. We tooled around town in that ride, cruising for action and girls. Occasionally, we double dated, and we had good times in that old car. As high school ended I was inducted into the National Honor Society and graduated among the top ten of my class of 300. In a way, I lived a double life, doing well on the outside but coping with a great fear of being taken from my home on the inside. At times it was overwhelming.

After the Rodriquez siblings left, Stanley and Alvin came and stayed for several years. These years were relatively happy ones. When Alvin was adopted he was replaced by Johnnie, who stayed with us for four months. He was "retarded", and was sent to a school for retarded children. Mom, Dad and I had really bonded with him, and it broke our hearts when he had to leave. I remember that he tried so hard to say my name, but he never could manage it. It seemed to me so unfair that he had to go. He was a good kid, and he tried so hard with everything. We all wept together at his departure.

Then Stanley's mother remarried, and Stanley went home. He was replaced by Ralph, who stayed with us for two years. He was adopted. Walter came after Stanley left. He was in bad shape. He had been abused. He arrived with the clothes he was wearing, and they were rags. He carried a paper bag, half full of worthless belongings. He was barely able to talk. He was only with us for three months, but in that time he made astounding progress and showed amazing resilience. I was 10 years old when he came, and became very involved with his learning. Mom asked me to teach him how to use the flatware, and he learned. She encouraged me to help him speak. I taught him how to ride a bike. We grew to love him way before the three-month departure. Again, it broke our hearts to see him go. He had to leave to go to a school for the mentally handicapped because he couldn't cope with a regular public school setting.

Stanley was followed by Kenneth, who was 12 while I was 11. He came to us very upset, because he was one of five brothers, and they'd been separated, and he missed his brothers very much. But he remembered where they lived. Even though it was against the rules for sibs from different foster homes to visit one another, Mom drove Kenneth over to where his brothers were. That was Mom. After this, he was able to settle down in our home. He was an avid reader, and a good long distance swimmer. He was with us for four years. The end came when he had an explosive encounter with the school principal. This man had a prosthetic arm, which Ken threatened to remove and hit him over the head with. He was sent to reform school. It was a traumatic loss. I was 15 when Ken left. He left me with a love of reading and swimming which has always remained with me.

After Ken left Ted came, and he was "trouble". He was 16 and I was 15. He had been to 12 previous foster homes, never staying very long at any of them. He once told me that he looked forward to moving to the next place. Inevitably, we clashed. Not too long after he arrived we had it out. I had a fairly large paper route, which gave me pocket money. I discovered that he was stealing my money, and I confronted him. It was outrage on the spot, and we had a huge, bare-fisted fight. Although he was a year older than I was we were the same weight and the same height, and we went at it. I remember Mom Hauck cheering me on. We kept slugging it out, and he hit my left upper arm and my cheekbone so hard that the blows tore the flesh off both spots. I responded by hitting him in the jaw and the blow knocked him off his feet. That was the end of the fight. Ted said later that he had never been knocked off his feet before, and that he was surprised and stunned to have it happen now. Ted and I had an uneasy truce then, but before long he ran away after being with us for three months. He was subsequently picked up on the NYC subway system and taken to a reform school.

Johnny came after Ted was gone. He was eight and I was 15. After being with us about six months he was seriously injured by an automobile and hospitalized for the next nine months. He returned to us and had a noticeable limp, but he made a remarkable recovery.

When we boys were young, temper flare-ups and misbehavior seemed easily handled. Mom and Dad neither believed in nor used corporal punishment, and they meted out "just rewards" with fairness and firmness and temperance when we misbehaved.

But as my round with Ted shows, there were times, as we got older, when things got rough, and Mom and Dad felt they had to control us and enforce the rules. They developed a way to do this that I still vividly remember. Dad made a strap out of a single piece of leather. It was about 16 inches long. One end was shaped like a handle and the other end had four or five 12-inch tails cut into it. If one of us got into trouble the guilty one had to lower his pants and underwear, lean over a stool and be whipped with that strap. These "whippings" were memorable and sometimes severe.

I hated these whippings because they not only hurt, they were shaming and humiliating and infuriating. Although I cried out in pain, I couldn't express my anger or rage because if I did I knew that I "could lose my happy home". Mom seldom used those chilling words, and then only when she was at her wits end. But they always carried a lot of frightening, terrifying emotional weight. Finally there came a day when I decided: this has got to stop! The only thing I could think of was to resolve not to yell when that strap hit my buttocks. Luckily, the next whipping was not severe, and I was able to keep my resolve. Thereafter the whippings stopped for everyone.

Before they stopped, though, Mom told me not to swim in a sandpit quarry hole because a boy had recently drowned there. I disobeyed and went swimming in the quarry hole. When she found out about it she was enraged. She cornered me in the basement and beat the living daylights out of me with a short rubber hose. She lost it. I had welts all over my body. I still remember the pain of it.

Much later I was able to understand her motivation. She was desperately trying to be protective of me, and she feared for my life. She wanted to control my risky behavior. But surely there had to be a better way to do it.

As an adult, as I reflect back upon these events, I realize that today this kind of parental behavior would be considered emotional and physical abuse, and of course, it was. But I sympathize with her now, and I know she was driven to this kind of punishment by stress and overload. But that doesn't excuse it.

I also realized that the times of departure of the foster boys were very painful and heartbreaking for my mom, too. She was determined to do all she could to prevent any of us from being taken away. As we got older, she thought the beatings were a way to keep control. Sadly, she was wrong.

The summer I was 14 I wanted to take a hitchhiking trip around New England. I wanted to get to each of the New England states. I also wanted to see what it would be like to get away from the home that I both loved and feared. I wanted a taste of being on my own, of being in control of my own life and not being subject to the caprices of my foster brothers who came and went, creating such emotional upset in me. I also wanted to be free of Mom Hauck, who I dearly loved but who also held so much power over me.

Amazingly, Mom let me go.

One evening after hitchhiking all day I went to a village police station and jail to see if I could sleep there for the night. A policeman took my name, address and phone number and called Mom to see if I was a runaway. She told him she was aware of my trip and sanctioned it, and he gave me shelter for the night., There was something a little unnerving about the whole experience. It turned out I was glad I did it because it gave me a feeling of self-reliance, and a move toward some more inner strength. I had tried my wings, but I was still glad to get home.

DAD STEWART DIES: APRIL 15, 1951

Dad Stewart died on April 15, 1951. He was 71 and I was fifteen and a half. He had a stroke and was in a coma for about two weeks. Mom Hauck cared for him in our home the whole time. Surprisingly, his dying there was not terribly traumatic for me. I had time to prepare myself emotionally for his death and to grow to accept the fact that this kindly old man's life was over. I grieved, but I was not knocked off my pins.

But the fact of his death was frightening and emotionally paralyzing because I thought that now, with Dad gone, there would be no father in the home and I would be placed in that dreaded "next home". The familiar fear gripped me. During the rest of my sophomore year my grades fell and I went from being the clean-up batter, batting fourth, to being the eighth batter on our junior varsity baseball team. The threat seemed enormous. I thought that I had figured out a way to stay in this home: by being both a good student and a good kid. Maybe that wasn't going to be enough.

The next several months were tense ones for me. What would happen to me? And then someone decided that I would stay with Mom Hauck until I graduated from high school. The relief that news brought to me was tremendous!

FATHER RETURNS TO PUERTO RICO: 1951

The autumn following Dad Stewart's death my father visited me and told me that he was leaving NYC to return to Puerto Rico permanently. Finances were an issue. He felt hounded by the foster care agency requesting money for my support. He had hoped to earn enough money to send me to college, he said, and then he told me that Mom Hauck had told him that I wanted to put myself through college. He said she said that I had been saving since I was seven years old and that I had saved enough for four years of college.

I was incredulous. This, of course, was impossible and a rather absurd fabrication. I'm not sure to this day where it came from. He also told me that the foster care agency psychiatrist had told him that his visits upset me, and he thought it best for me if he left. He felt free to go because I was in such a good home. We said goodbye, and as it turned out, I would not see him again for 17 years.

Fernando Leaves Home: 1953

After Dad Stewart died and my father returned to Puerto Rico, Johnny was still with us, and then Dennis came in July of 1952. When I left for college in the fall of 1953 both Johnny, who had been with us three years, and Dennis, who was with us a year, left for other foster homes.

Leaving for college turned out to be difficult for me on a number of levels. The most obvious one was that I knew that my leaving would mean that Johnny and Dennis would have to leave too. Mom relied on me to help with the younger ones, and I would be gone. Her years as a foster mother were coming to an end.

Also, I had formed a very deep and powerful attachment to this woman who had been my foster mother. I was the only one of her foster children who managed, with her love and support, and because of the particular circumstances of my parents' lives, to stay with her over the years. Both Mom and I knew, and were told repeatedly by the foster care agency over the years, that when I graduated from high school I would be on my own.

I did graduate from high school in June of 1953, and my being on my own was formalized the following September 3rd when I was "discharged to my own responsibility" from the Sheltering Arms Children's Service and the NYC Welfare Department and became financially responsible for myself.

The spring before I graduated good fortune had come to me in the person of Ward Owen who was my high school guidance counselor. He had helped me research college options, and I had come up with a final choice of two: Muskingum College in Ohio and Blackburn College in Illinois. I chose Blackburn, which was a work-study school, and had a good academic rating as well. So when the fall of '53 came, with the combination of some savings from part-time work, some scholarship assistance and the work-study plan at Blackburn, I headed out.

But leaving home pushed my need to know more about my biological family. It felt like I was being cast out into the world with no formal ties to anyone, and the prospect was scary and more than a little daunting.

MOM HAUCK'S TRUNK: 1953

When I left to go to college Mom did a wonderful thing: she gave me the steamer trunk that she had carried her clothes and belongings in when she emigrated to the U.S. from Switzerland. With that trunk, one of her prized possessions, she gave me part of herself and her history. This gracious gift solidified and strengthened our connection without a word being said. Even though I was discharged from her care, I knew our tie would remain strong.

I remained in touch with Mom by writing letters to her and by visiting her for Christmas and Easter holidays. I stayed in touch with her for the rest of her life and to this day I cherish her trunk. But even more than that I cherish the gift of Mom's, and Dad's, mostly patient, and always encouraging and steadfast love.

~ COLLEGE AND MARRIAGE ~
FERNANDO: 1953-1968

AN UNSETTLING EXPERIENCE

I was unable to find work the summer before I left for college, so two high school friends, Jim Schuck and Art Hedler, and I decided to ride to Seattle, Washington with Jim's older brother who was returning to an army base. The plan was for the three of us to go to Seattle with him and then hitchhike down the West Coast and back across the southwest, me to college in Illinois and they on back to Long Island.

We had a great time doing just that. We made it to Arkansas, and were heading to our respective destinations when the fun ended. We couldn't get a ride in Arkansas. We decided to split up and meet at the Greyhound station in Memphis, Tennessee. They got rides but I didn't. I had to walk to the next town; it was midnight when I arrived. I was exhausted, so I decided to sleep on the grass in a park, which was located in the center square of the town. Soon two policemen interrupted my sleep. They checked my I.D. and the amount of money in my wallet. Since I had a small amount of money, they declared me a vagrant, put me in their squad car and took me to the jail. When we arrived there they pushed me up a long flight of dark stairs, opened an iron gate, marched me down a corridor, opened another iron gate, shoved me in a large unlighted cell and slammed the door behind me. My requests to make a phone call were ignored. Once in the unlighted cell I heard someone breathing heavily in his sleep. I knew then that I was not alone, but I had, of course, no idea who this other person might be. You can imagine the fright.

I crept along a rail wall, found a metal ledge along it, and sat with my back to the hallway outside the cell, staying wide awake, ready for whatever might happen next. At daybreak I found that the person in the cell with me was a man in his late 20's who was jailed for drunk driving. It was a Saturday. For the rest of that day, and all of Sunday, I sat imprisoned with this man, "freaking out" and wondering what was going to happen to me.

Finally, early Monday morning, a cleaning lady came to clean the hall and I appealed to her to talk to someone in the police station about my situation. She promised to do so, and within minutes I was escorted out of the cell and into an office where there was a young man who appeared to be an attorney. He told me that I was picked up and jailed for being a vagrant because I had less that $5 in my wallet. He also said there'd been a murder in the area, and the police noticed that I had a red spot on my shirt (red paint from painting for Mom before I left) and they thought it might be blood. He ignored my complaint about not getting to make a phone call and my story about trying to get to college. Instead, without any explanation, he had me escorted to the street and I was set free.

I was still in a huge quandary. I was unshaven and unkempt. I'd lost my small traveling bag in the misadventure. I'd become deeply tanned over the summer and was quite dark. I noticed with shock and fear that there were drinking fountains and toilets for "colored only" and I wondered if that might be me. I thought: man, I've got to get out of here as fast as I can! I went to the bus station and discovered that I had just enough money to get out of Arkansas. I figured that by now Jim and Art had arrived in Memphis, so I took the bus to Memphis. I found out later that they had waited for me for a day, and when I didn't arrive they went on home, assuming that I would go on to school in Illinois. It was about time for school to start.

After escaping from Arkansas I hitchhiked to central Illinois and Blackburn. I slept one night in an old car in a salvage yard, and a second night in a farmer's hayloft. The farmer and his wife were amazing. I had asked permission to sleep in their barn, which they gave, and then they fed me a huge breakfast in the morning. I hadn't eaten for three days. I can't even think of a word strong enough to express my gratitude for that breakfast! They also found a ride for me to Carlinville and Blackburn College. Thanks to the farmer, I was able to shave that morning, but I still looked disheveled and unkempt. Later, when I graduated from Blackburn, I took Mom Hauck back to meet the farmer and his wife. Mom felt as appreciative of their hospitality to me as I did. We had a wonderful time visiting with them.

As I arrived on campus I got very, very strange looks because of my appearance. I was able to establish my identity as an incoming student and the man in the administration office was able to suppress his shock and unease. He directed me to the dorm room where Mom Hauck's trunk had been delivered. It was a reassuring sight. What a way to start my college career!

MY COLLEGE CAREER BEGINS: 1953

Blackburn College is located near cornfields outside of Carlinville, Illinois, a small farming town situated fifty miles south of Springfield, Illinois and fifty miles north of St. Louis, Missouri. There was no theater in town, and the only source of entertainment that was available was what we could create when we went to the "Wonder Bar", and believe me, it was no wonder bar!

Blackburn was (and is) a small Presbyterian college with a strong liberal arts and science curriculum. It was a unique place; at the time it had a student body of about 300. It was also a work-study college where all students, without exception, had to work 15 hours a week. The work-plan was considered to be an integral part of the students' education. Since everyone worked, I didn't feel like odd-man-out. I began my studies there as a biology/pre-med major. Fortunately, I did well. My major professor, Dr. William Werner, was excellent. He was also a mentor and a friend.

MY FATHER: 1953

When I went to college my father and I maintained an erratic correspondence, which enabled us to keep a thin connection. That first year at BU I was feeling the absence of family and I began to ask my father more specific questions: about himself, about his family and about my mother and about her family. It was in this way that I learned that my father was one of 14 siblings, ten who lived, and that I had five aunts and four uncles, and numerous cousins. I also learned that my mother's name was Margarita López. I had always thought of her as "my mother". I was astonished to realize I hadn't even known her name. Later I learned that most of my uncles lived their lives in Puerto Rico, and all my aunts immigrated to the U.S. and returned to Puerto Rico when they retired. Puerto Rico was extremely hard-hit by the depression of 1929, and there were more opportunities for my aunts in the U.S. My uncles were able to continue to farm or find modest jobs on the island. My father, however, sought a better life for himself by joining the army.

Mom Hauck: Christmas Holiday 1953

Christmas Holiday came that first year, and I returned home to Elmont and Mom Hauck. I got a job delivering mail. I was glad I was home. During that vacation period I came down with a severe strep throat, with swelling that made breathing difficult. Mom was very alarmed and made me go to bed. She called a doctor, who came to the house, gave me antibiotics and demanded bed rest. I was one sick person!

Mom was very worried and sat by my bed, weeping quietly. I will always remember that time, because it told me that in spite of it all, in spite of the fear we both had to struggle with – my fear of being taken away and having to leave her and her fear of having to give me up – our bond was permanent. She loved me deeply, and that love endured.

One day after I had recovered I said, "Mom, you have been so good to me, what can I ever do to repay you?" She looked at me with her wonderful smile and said, "Just be good to other people." To this day, there are times when I am praying or meditating when I see her smiling at me with that radiance. What a source of strength, beauty and love she was to me, and continues to be.

Lois Jane Crump Enters My Life: 1955

In the spring of 1955, prior to my junior year in college, Lois Jane Crump, who was a cousin of a classmate and friend of mine, came to Blackburn for a prospective-student visit. Her tour group was visiting the library, and she saw me checking out some books. We made fleeting eye contact, and she told me later that in that instant she knew I was the man she was going to marry. Strange!

As her group left the library and went into the adjoining hall, full of 17-year-old enthusiasm, she mentioned to a friend who was with her that she had just seen the man she was going to marry. I had always been flattered that she singled me out, but was also a little skeptical of this story. But my mathematics professor, Dr. Bretthauer, who was just entering the library at the time the group was leaving, remembers hearing the comment, or as he said later, "the announcement". He remembers glancing at the excited girl and smiling at the exuberance of youth! He told me this story when Lois and I returned to BU for my class' 25th reunion.

A few months after this brief encounter, at the beginning of summer, I hitchhiked all over Western Europe with my friend Jack Greenshields. Jack was a classmate of mine at Blackburn. He was a fun loving guy and we became very good friends. We hitchhiked all over Western Europe that summer of 1955. We slept in fields, police stations, on fire escapes, and occasionally, in youth hostels. Every day was a new adventure because we never knew where we would be or who we would be with the next day. It was a wonderful, carefree summer and Jack and I reveled in it.

Back at Blackburn in September, I began my junior year with renewed vigor. I played on the intramural football team and was enjoying once again the antics of dorm life. It was a particularly beautiful autumn in central Illinois, and spirits were high all over campus.

Lois Crump did indeed matriculate with the incoming freshman class. I remember noticing her, not only because she was attractive and because she was my friend Don Detwiler's cousin (and Don did introduce us), but also because it seemed like every guy I knew was asking her out. I was intrigued, but I was not persuaded to follow suit. Nevertheless, her sparkling blue eyes, her brown hair, her great warm smile, and the way she carried herself made her hard to ignore.

Much to my amazement, around the first part of October I kept running into Lois everywhere. She will tell you herself that she pursued me shamelessly, and there's mischief in her eyes at the telling! It still makes me smile. Finally, I asked her to take a walk one rainy October evening and we walked and walked, soaking up the autumn beauty that that evening held. She was easy to talk to: intelligent, sensitive and full of joy and life. When we got back to her dorm I wanted to kiss her goodnight, which was sort of standard procedure in 1955 when you took your girl back to her dorm at the 10PM curfew. The trouble was, there were dozens of other couples standing in that dorm lobby, too, and everyone was saying goodnight. It was awkward.

I was holding Lois' red raincoat, and it occurred to me to toss it over both our heads: our own private haven for a few minutes. I kissed her and she kissed me back. It was electric for me, because she <u>really</u> kissed me! She invited me to the campus Sadie Hawkins dance, and then to her home in Springfield, Illinois for the Thanksgiving Holiday.

The visit to Lois' home for the Thanksgiving weekend was a very positive experience. I was warmly welcomed by Lois' mother, father, and younger sister, Jan, and some of Lois' friends. Her parents lived in a middle class neighborhood in a nice home. I could immediately sense and experience that Lois came from a very warm and loving family. Her father was an engineer, and her mother was a musician and a teacher. I just knew that they were very solid people who had created a very good home for their daughters.

When I entered their home I could see that it was beautifully decorated. There was a formal arrangement of upholstered furniture placed around a fireplace. There was lush green carpeting on the living and dining room floors, and the windows were tastefully curtained. There was a nicely appointed dining room, with a large table and matching chairs. The whole home had a wonderful quality of pleasantness, tastefulness and serenity, and it was a delight to the eye.

We had a wonderful Thanksgiving dinner together. The table was set with lovely china, crystal and silver. The meal was served in courses, and though formal, an air of fun and joy prevailed. The cooking rivaled Mom Hauck's! The family was very gracious and hospitable to me, and we had a very good first visit.

I must confess, though, that I couldn't help but wonder what they really thought about this tall, dark and heavily bearded young man from New York. I was also very aware that Lois and I came from very different family experiences. I also knew I was very attracted to her and the kind of family life she came from. It was exciting!

After that, Lois and I spent all our spare time together. Then I left for a spring break trip, and ended up cutting it short to return to Springfield to see Lois. I hitched back, and we had agreed that she'd pick me up on the edge of town where my ride would most probably let me off. I phoned her at my arrival. I watched her car approach our meeting spot, but I was totally unprepared for the joy of having her fly into my arms, with hugs of welcome, eyes shining and face aglow. It was the powerful magic you hear about, and I was experiencing it!

Our relationship developed quickly. By March we knew we wanted to be married. Lois called her older sister, Jean, with the news, we told her parents and younger sister, Jan, and soon wedding plans were underway. Since I was not yet 21 and from out-of-state I had to get Mom Hauck's permission to be married. She had to sign an affidavit. She was not happy; in fact, she was upset and angry. She'd thought I would marry a "nice German girl". Finally she consented to sign. But she did not attend the wedding.

Our Wedding: 1956

We were married June 9, 1956 at the Douglas Avenue Methodist Church in Springfield, Illinois. It was the end of Lois' freshman year and the end of my junior year. She was not quite 19 and I was not quite 21. In retrospect, it was amazing: we had no financial base whatsoever. We were both still in school. I had $200 in a savings account and Lois had no savings account at all.

The afternoon of our 8PM wedding, while all of the women in Lois' family were scrambling around in preparation, I lay in the Crump's back yard on a blanket on the lawn, and napped. I felt totally calm, peaceful and serene about the whole situation. I knew I was marrying into a good and kind family: caring of one another and other people, connected to each other and to their extended families, participating in their community and committed to the larger world. Lois had two sisters: her sister Jean was married to Bill Carr, her sister Jan was still in high school. It was a closely knit family. They included me as one of their own. It was a very wonderful family for me to become a part of.

As I said before, Mom was angry with me for my decision to marry and did not attend the wedding. This was very disappointing to me; I wanted her to be there. Only two people from my life in New York came: two high school friends, Larry Rauchut and Don Bouchard. All the rest of the guests were Lois' family, her friends, our college friends and my biology professor, Dr. Werner, and his wife. Jack Greenshields, my college friend and hitchhiking buddy was my best man; Lois' older sister Jean was her matron of honor. Her youngest sister Jan was one of her attendants. After a happy reception in the pavilion of a park close to Lois' home, one of the favorite places of her childhood, we left for our honeymoon: 10 days in the Ozark Mountains.

As we were leaving town (it must have been nearly midnight) we both wanted to go back to Douglas Church. In those days, churches could be left unlocked 24/7 and so we did. We entered the darkened building and saw that the nave was dimly lit and so we walked down the center aisle a second time that day and knelt at the altar. We didn't speak for a long time. We found out later that the fervent prayer in both of our minds and hearts was that God would bless this marriage. We've been married 46 years and blessings have indeed abounded. We have butted heads a thousand times but we have rarely, if ever, butted hearts.

Marrying Lois turned out to be the singularly best decision I've ever made. But blessed as our marriage was, it wasn't easy. Our backgrounds were so different: socially, culturally and racially. Our faith has been the foundation of our strength as a couple. We've had some good individual, couple and family therapy to help put it altogether. We also had incredible support from Lois' family, and were fortunate to develop, from early in our marriage and all along the years, deep and abiding friendships: each of us as individuals, as a couple and with other families. We had abundant times of joy and celebration and some tough times as well. And always, we had the support of family and friends. This time, as opposed to childhood, it was the joy and wonder of it all that was overwhelming! The love that Lois has given me has been profound, unwavering and truly steadfast. Her continuing love has gifted, grounded, graced and blessed me unfailingly.

GRADUATION FROM BLACKBURN: 1957

The fall after our wedding Lois and I returned to Blackburn for her sophomore year and my senior year. In June 1957 I graduated, with a major in biology. Lois finished her sophomore year. When her parents discussed with her her decision to marry they asked her to promise to finish her college education She promised, and she kept that promise. Generously, Dad and Mom Crump continued to pay for all her educational expenses.

Graduation day was a happy time for us. Dad and Mom Crump were there, and Mom Hauck came from New York to help us celebrate the occasion. It was the first time Mom Hauck met Lois, and Lois' parents. We all had a wonderful weekend together.

VOCATIONAL DECISIONS: 1957

During my last two years at Blackburn I struggled with the issue of what to do with my life, what vocation to follow. I was a pre-med student and did well academically, but after much soul searching and a visit with a friend who was in medical school, the idea of becoming a doctor no longer seemed right. I then considered the ministry but after doing some reading and visiting a couple of seminaries I knew that wasn't right for me either. What I did know was that I wanted to work with people in one way or another. But I couldn't figure out what it was going to be. Later, I found psychology fascinating and I began reading a psychology text. I came upon a one-paragraph description of what clinical psychologists do: talk to people with problems and enter into a process with them called psychotherapy. The words leapt off the page. Suddenly it clicked: this is what I wanted to do. Much later I came to understand that becoming a clinical psychologist was a natural extension of my childhood experience when, with Mom Hauck's and Dad Stewart's example, I was so involved in trying to help my foster brothers grow up in positive ways so that their lives would be positive ones.

So I applied to a dozen different graduate programs in clinical psychology. I hoped that with this shotgun approach I would get accepted someplace. I had not taken one undergraduate psychology course. Spring semester of my senior year came and all the rejection letters came as well. I was stymied. After graduation we located to North Chicago where I could get work as a laborer until I figured out what I was going to do.

I was faced too with the reality that I had to address my obligation to military service. I had been given a college deferment by my draft board at the time of my enrollment at BU. So I opted for a program that required six months of active duty followed by six and a half years of inactive duty. I applied for the program, passed the mental and physical tests and was accepted.

The day before I was to report for duty, I received a piece of mail that was to change the course of my life. It was a letter from the admissions office of the graduate school at Michigan State University, offering a provisional acceptance to the graduate psychology program for the fall of 1957. I was astounded! Maybe even more astounding at that point was that my draft board, on this moment's notice, granted permission for me to continue my studies. Instead of me reporting for duty the next day, Lois and I began to make plans to move to East Lansing.

We arrived at MSU in late August 1957. We were in for some culture shock. We had come from a small college campus of 300 to a large university of 20,000. When we went to the first home football game at Spartan Stadium, we felt somewhat lost in that sea of humanity. But it didn't take us long to get into the swing of things. We adapted quickly to this Big Ten university: it was an exciting and stimulating place to be. I settled in to study psychology and Lois settled in to study anthropology, social science and English/American literature.

I was admitted to MSU on a provisional basis, and the proviso was that I would take the requisite set of undergraduate psychology courses, and do well in them. Then I would be formally accepted into their graduate program in clinical psychology. I did well and I was accepted, but the provisional semesters were a challenge. I was required to take general psychology, experimental psychology, statistics, and tests and measurement. It all seemed to have nothing to do with people. It seemed like I was studying rat psychology, not human psychology. The frustration of it all became enormous. With Lois' wonderful love and support I persevered, and eventually I did indeed move on to the clinical courses and the formal degree program in Clinical Psychology.

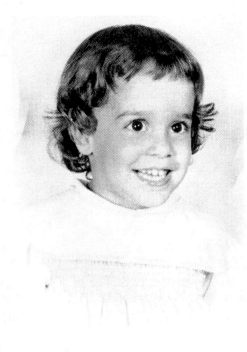

KATHLEEN IS BORN: 1958

At the beginning of our second year at MSU our first child, Kathleen, was born on September 22, 1958. This was an over-the-top happy event for Lois and me. Lois was thrilled to have a child and I was stunned by this birth. When I first held Kathleen I couldn't believe how tiny she was, how beautiful she was and how perfect she was! Her skin was darker, too; darker than Lois' – a bit like me. It was a stunning experience for me and all the more profound because now, for the first time in my life, I was a part of my own biological family. That's very different from being part of a foster family where I always felt different from other people who came from their own families.

MORE FAMILY INFORMATION: 1958

When we sent Kathleen's birth announcement to my father I asked him more questions about my Puerto Rican extended families. I wanted to be more connected to them and to have Lois and Kathleen more connected to them as well. I learned again that my father had nine siblings, four brothers and five sisters, and that his mother was now 83 years old. He said he had 24 aunts and uncles, all of them small farmers living in Puerto Rico. He told me considerably less about my mother's family. He said she was raised by an uncle and that she had a younger sister who was a widow with three children. He told me that her Uncle Isaac visited me at Mom Hauck's foster home with the sister's youngest son who was about my age. I was about 7 or 8 at the time. (It was the older man, Isaac, who took my picture with Butch!) He also said that he and my mother met and married in NYC in 1934. It was very significant to me to get this family information. Now Lois and I could begin to locate Kathleen and ourselves within the context of my biological family. It was satisfying.

Gregory Martin Is Born: 1961

I continued my graduate studies and Lois continued taking courses toward her undergraduate degree. Our lives were full to the top: marveling at and enjoying Kathleen, attending classes, studying, spending time with friends. These busy years were rich ones. Then on March 24, 1961 our second child and first son, Gregory Martin, was born. We were elated at his birth. He was a beautiful, already handsome, robust, brown-eyed baby and we fell in love with him instantly. He was going to favor Lois' side of the family, we thought.

Internship At Topeka State Hospital: 1961

In July 1961 we moved from East Lansing to Topeka, Kansas. I was accepted into a 12-month full time clinical psychology internship at Topeka State Hospital, which was affiliated with the Menniger School of Psychiatry's training program. Now I was, certainly, working with people. This program was very intense: I rotated through the adult-male and adult-female inpatient's services as well as the adult outpatient service.

Graduation From Michigan State University: 1963

After the internship year in Topeka, we all returned to MSU where Lois and I finished our studies. We graduated at the Fall Commencement 1963, I with my Ph.D. and Lois with her B.A. Lois' family attended the ceremony: her parents, Jean and husband Bill, and Jan. Another person came also: Mom Hauck! It was a singular event in our lives and we celebrated for several days with these dear people. Lois planned a big party and we filled our home with friends and laughter, and music as well. What a memorable time! Mom Hauck could barely contain her joy.

In January, I started a full time, one-year appointment with the MSU counseling Center. We rented a wonderful Dutch Colónial home on Victor Street in East Lansing on the Red Cedar River from a faculty couple who was on sabbatical. What a very happy year it was! I had completed the Ph.D. grind, I had a good job, and I also had time to be with Lois, Kathleen and Marty without distraction. I even had time to shop for a puppy, and brought one home hidden inside my coat on Valentine's Day: basset hound Victor Valentine. Life was unbelievably good!

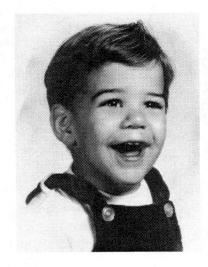

MATTHEW JOSEPH IS BORN: 1964

Following that year's appointment I accepted a job at Penn State University in State College, PA. It was here that our second son and last child, Matthew Joseph, was born on September 27, 1964. We were thrilled by his birth on that brilliant sunlit morning. He was a beautiful, vital, healthy, brown-eyed boy. He was a joy from the first second we saw him. Lois and I laughed with each other: this child looked to be a combination of both our families!

We now had three incredible children. We were sitting on top of the world!

MOVE TO NORTH CAROLINA: 1965

After a year at PSU I continued my career at the University of North Carolina, where I stayed from 1965 to 1970. We all loved Chapel Hill, with its friendly southern culture and charming ways. As I joined the faculty there, so did three other young psychologists and we became life-long friends. The four families began to celebrate Thanksgiving together, and the four of us, our wives and our children became fast friends. Eventually, three of us were offered good jobs elsewhere, and we got together for one last gathering. At one point during that evening there was an abrupt silence as we realized we were about to break up a wonderful group of friends. Our sadness was palpable. As we struggled with this reality I suggested that we make a commitment to spend the Thanksgiving weekend with each other every year. We agreed, and that is what

we have done for the last thirty-two years. At first we took turns going to one another's homes. Now our numbers have grown. Our children have grown, and now our children are bringing their children to these autumn celebrations. In recent years we've gathered at a state park lodge to accommodate our large group.

This has been a most satisfying and rewarding experience. In many ways we have become "family" for each other. Our children have been enriched by these experiences, and they think of the other couples as "aunts and uncles". The gathering at Thanksgiving continues to be a source of support, love and connection for us. For me, this experience was very related to my search for family. It enabled me to be a part of creating an extended family before I found and reconnected with my birth family.

We purchased our first home in 1966, a split-level on a lovely wooded lot in a neighborhood surrounded by acres of wonderful woodland. It was a perfect place for our children to wander and roam. All our student years we had lived in married student housing and rentals and duplexes, so the purchase of this home was a big milestone for us. Again, Lois' parents' generosity supported our desire to own our home: they loaned us the down payment to help get us started.

~ FERNANDO'S SEARCH FOR ~
FAMILY INFORMATION CONTINUES:
1965-1970

UNANSWERED QUESTIONS

When we moved to Chapel Hill in 1965 I was 30 years old and my career was well underway. I was happily married and we had three wonderful children. Still, I felt a lack of real, vital connection to my extended families in Puerto Rico. Throughout my high school, college and graduate school years my father and I had had the thinnest thread of correspondence. Within this correspondence I had slowly accumulated bits and pieces of information about my extended families. Even so I knew little more than the fact that my father came from a large family and that my mother came from a much smaller one, both in Puerto Rico.

While I was being raised by Mom Hauck and Dad Stewart my father had become a sergeant in the U.S. Army and was stationed at Fort Hayes in New Jersey. He would occasionally visit me. I remember being confused by his visits but also filled with curiosity. I was impressed by his impeccable uniform and regarded him with respect. Yet each of his visits brought up troubling questions I've mentioned before: who was I and to whom did I really belong?

It helped when my father's youngest sister, Luz, her husband Luis and their niece Iris visited me when I was an early teen. Their skin color, hair and eyes were the same color as mine! I felt the same way when my Aunt Berta, my father's sister, and her family visited. When the older man visited (who I later found out was my great-uncle Isaac) with the young boy the whole visit seemed a mystery to me. They didn't reveal who they were (which I later found out was my father's stipulation in allowing the visit). I remember being surprised at how very happy they were to see me. We visited in the living room while Mom served coffee and cookies. They asked to take some pictures of me, and that's when I posed in the backyard with my dog Butch. The experience was pleasant but it still left me with a strange sense of mystery. Who were these people?

Elementary school was a positive time for me, but there were hard times there as well, times that set me apart and deepened my confusion about who I was. When I was 10 years old my music teacher decided that my first name, Fernando, was too long. So he proceeded to give me a shorter, Anglicized name, and it stuck. The name he gave me was "Ferd". In front of the whole class he announced that my name would now be "Ferd"! I was unable to find words of protest as this insensitive man was wrenching my real name away from me. From then on the other teachers, my classmates, my friends and sometimes even my foster family called me "Ferd". Once again I experienced a sense of loss and diminishment. This time it carried with it a feeling of embarrassment and humiliation.

Years later, after I had been married for about 15 years, the memory of the music teacher who had so cavalierly ripped my name from me enraged me. I decided to reclaim my name: Fernando. It was not easy to do. Lois, especially had a hard time. She had fallen in love with me as "Ferd" and she had known me for 16 years with that name. But gradually she, my family, and my friends and colleagues made the switch. These days, our three grandchildren call me Nando, a common Hispanic nickname for Fernando. I like it; it has a nice ring and a warm quality to it.

Even though as a child, adolescent and young adult I had lost my Puerto Rican first name, I relished the Hispanic fact of my last name: Colón. During one of my father's visits with me he took great care to explain the importance of putting an accent over the last "o" of Colón. If I didn't, he warned, people would confuse my name with the large intestine, and that would not be good. I consider this one of my father's most important and precious gifts to me. He gave me very few gifts as the years unfolded, but this gift of my name turned out to be a big one for me. By emphasizing how I was to pronounce my name he instilled in me a sense of pride about my name and my heritage. Every time I accented that "o" I felt a connection to him and to my family lineage.

This sense of connection was enhanced further when Mom Hauck insisted that I take Spanish when languages were offered in high school, and not German, her native tongue. I don't know if she was advised by the caseworker to do so or not, but she honored my Spanish ancestry by insisting that I take Spanish. This was very significant and important to me.

One day I brought out the letters from my father that I'd accumulated. In response to my questioning about my mother and biological family, the foster care agency had also written to me during the previous 16 years. I had saved every letter from my father and the agency. I decided to lay all this correspondence out in sequence on the floor to see if I could make more sense out of it. As I put the pieces together from these letters it became clear to me that some of my father's letters contained inconsistencies and that the agency was telling a different story than my father was. I was convinced that neither of them was telling me the full story even though I had tried repeatedly to get the full story from both of them. It also began to dawn on me that my father's answers to my questions were not only inconsistent but that he might be withholding truth from me as well.

I decided that the time had come for me to visit Puerto Rico in order to re-establish a face-to-face contact with my father. I wanted to see if I could learn more about my families firsthand.

SOME ANSWERS: PUERTO RICO TRIP #1 — 1968

I made my first trip to Puerto Rico with Lois and our children in 1968. I was 33 years old, Lois was 31 and the children were 10, 7 and 4. It had been 17 years since I had last seen my father, when I was 16. I felt both excitement and anxiety at the prospect of our meeting again. I wasn't sure how we would get along after such a long separation. He had little knowledge about what my adult life had become. He hadn't met Lois or our children. I wondered how such a visit would go. Could my father and I pick up where we left off? I wondered if such a thing was possible but I thought it was worth a try. We had read about Puerto Rico in preparation for the trip. We knew of its beauty, its poverty, its progress and its problems. We were ready to go.

As we approached the island I was straining to bring it into focus through the window of the plane. From the air, at a distance, it looked like a green jewel surrounded by waters of amazing colors – deep azure far out, gradually becoming clear, almost translucent turquoise close to shore. As the plane dropped a little in altitude I could see the white/gold ribbon that is the beach. Whitecaps were breaking far out from shore, turning into foamy waves as they hit the sand.

Then I saw the houses, packed close together, then San Juan and beyond, the green of the mountains. I remember steamy heat and the hot sun on my face as we exited the plane and walked across the sticky tarmac. And it <u>smelled</u> different: the mingling smells of jet fuel, the ocean, and the sweet smell of flowers. Suddenly we were enveloped by people – so many of them, mostly dark-skinned, laughing and crying and hugging as they greeted each other, all the while speaking rapid-fire Spanish, using their hands for emphasis. I thought of another Island, Long Island where I had grown up; how stunningly different Puerto Rico seemed!

When my father responded to my letter of inquiry about the visit he told me that he had remarried and included a recent photo of himself with his wife, Lydia. With the help of this photo we were able to recognize each other at the airport. My father said he saw me and wanted to rush and grab me, but he decided to wait to see if I recognized him first. Our greeting all around was warm and genuine. We seemed to have immediate rapport with Lydia, even though we spoke not a word of Spanish and she spoke not a word of English! My father looked great and he was quite spontaneous and warm-hearted. He joked a lot and seemed much more relaxed than I

had remembered him. He was 66 years old at this meeting. He said the kids looked quite Latin, and that he would have recognized the two boys anywhere. Lydia and Matt, our youngest, made up to each other right away. All the children soon agreed that they liked Grandma and Grandpa Colón.

As we left the airport I remember the traffic, including lots of horn honking and death-defying lane changes. Lush tropical growth was everywhere: palm trees, vines and endless flowers. I saw high rise luxury hotels, and not far from the busy highway I saw two people crouched in a cardboard box. I assumed that's where they were staying. There were stray dogs, and trash.

There were immaculately kept streets. There was unfamiliar, happy music spilling out of roadside bars and passing cars. There was a beat in the air, and I liked it.

Travel Misadventures In San Juan

We hadn't been invited to stay at my father's house for our visit. I imagine he and Lydia were a little leery of an unknown family of five as houseguests! We stayed our first night in the old Normandy Hotel in San Juan. The guidebook had misled us. The Normandy was more than a little run down and Lois was appalled and frightened. At first she refused to check in. I thought it wasn't great, but I also thought it wasn't impossible. When my father helped carry our baggage up to our room he warned us not to leave it unattended in our room, explaining that ex-hotel workers have skeleton keys that they used to rob the rooms. He also warned us not to go out at night because there were addicts and thieves in the neighborhood. All this was useful information but it was not an auspicious beginning for staying in this tropical paradise! Fortunately, he said he'd pick us up at 11 the following morning. We were already looking forward to that hour!

The room was unkempt and had no air conditioning and it was a very hot and humid July night. After my father left us, we pushed the heavy furniture against the door for safety and settled in for the night, although Lois and I were wondering what in the world we were going to do trapped in this unsavory hotel room with three little kids.

About that time Matt discovered the bidet and when he turned on the spigot we had a minor flood on our hands. The water shot up to the ceiling, spread evenly across it and began to drip, systematically soaking the entire room. At first we were upset with Matt, but how could he have known the consequences of turning that handle? As we began to clean up the mess we started to laugh, and ended up laughing so hard we could hardly stop. The tension was broken! It had been a long and challenging day and a good laugh was just what we needed.

Our 10 year old Kathleen was fascinated with the whole thing. She tells me now that she remembers the hotel as cavernous and shabby, but she thought it was cool. She slept in a tiny alcove off the bathroom. The walls were cracked and peeling. She kept waking up to stand on her bed to look out the window. The street below was busy and noisy. She couldn't wait, she says, to get out there and see what was going on.

Family Information And Ties With My Father's Extended Family

My father and Lydia arrived promptly at 11 the next morning. They took us to nearby El Morro, an old Spanish fort, and to the governor's mansion. We saw a few other sights and then went to their home in Guaynabo, a suburb of San Juan. They lived in a very pleasant three-bedroom house on a small lot in a nice neighborhood where all the homes were well kept and the lawns were nicely manicured. We stayed with them for the rest of our three-week visit. We made a number of visits to various parts of the island to meet members of my father's family and to see the sights.

As our visit unfolded we learned that Lydia and my father were married in 1952 when he was 50 years old and she was 19. Lydia was an orphan and was raised by an adoptive family. She was 35 when we met her. She turned out to be an "angel" in the story of my reconnection to my family.

I also learned that my father had been married to a Puerto Rican woman in NYC from 1944-1951. She had a son, and when my father returned to Puerto Rico she didn't want to return, and so he went alone. Once in Aibonito his mother told him about Lydia, an 18-year-old girl who lived in town and who she thought would be a good wife. Gregorio arranged to meet her. She made a meal for him and any doubts were set aside! Within six months they were married. My father had been ill while he was in the service and was subsequently unable to have children which was a disappointment to them both. They tried to adopt but couldn't because of my father's age.

As conversation unfolded with my father during our stay I got family information a little bit at a time. One of the first things I found out was that my paternal great-grandfather had been married twice, the second time at age 66. His first wife had borne 9 children before her death and his second wife had 9 children, too. My grandfather was in the second batch. My grandfather and grandmother had 14 children themselves, ten of who lived, and my father was one of them. As we talked about the family history my father told me that our "predominant lineage is Spanish with island Native Indian, and who knows, maybe some black blood as well".

My father took his two-week vacation from Wells Fargo where he was a guard so he could be with us during our visit. He took us around the island to meet the members of his family. The middle week Lois and I and the children explored the island on our own, and at the end of that time we treated ourselves to a night at the first class El Convento Hotel in Old San Juan. We invited my father and Lydia for dinner. The evening was enchanting: superb paella, accomplished Flamenco dancing as entertainment, and meaningful but light-hearted conversation with one another. I'll never forget it.

As we continued to get to know each other after what had been pretty much a 17-year cut-off, I discovered that my father read the daily newspaper. Our politics was similar and our opinions overlapped. Our conversations had substance. I was pleased. He still enjoyed dancing and singing, and he joked around a lot. I enjoyed his vitality.

As we continued to meet my paternal aunts, uncles and cousins I began to feel a tangible sense of connection to my father and Lydia, and to my father's extended family. My deep sense of disconnection began to fade. I felt that these feelings of connection, satisfaction, a sense of family pride and rootedness were at last taking the edge off my basic uncertainty about family that I had carried all my life.

I began to get some more detail. My father said that his grandfather was a tall, blue-eyed blond. This grandfather's second wife brought in "dark blood, a shade darker than olive". So there is indeed a mixture of Spanish, island-Indian and African blood in our family tree. I had always been interested in the genetic mix.

DISCOVERY AND REVELATION IN AIBONITO

We then spent a day traveling to and from my father's hometown of Aibonito. He had two brothers living there, my Uncle Jenaro and my Uncle Domingo. My father wanted me to see where he was born. It was quite a trip from the outskirts of San Juan, up winding mountain roads full of endless hairpin curves, sheer drop-offs, no guard rails, and little white crosses at the roadside marking the many spots where unlucky travelers had died. The vegetation grew thick and lush the higher we climbed. We passed through narrow-streeted villages where we saw shops with butchered whole pigs and chickens hanging just feet from the car windows. We saw what I took to be greengrocers. We passed shacks that were bars, with music blaring. There was the sweet coolness now of the mountain air, and along the way we stopped to look at a wonderful waterfall. We also stopped at a roadside stand where Grandpa Colón bought the children bags full of freshly cooked pig cracklings and rough, hairy whole coconuts with a straw inserted in a hole so they could drink the coconut milk.

Finally, we arrived in Aibonito and my father's birthplace. The original modest farmhouse had been rebuilt many times after hurricanes. Originally it had a kitchen and an eating area in one half while the other half of the house had a parental bedroom and curtain-divided space: one side for the boys and the other for the girls.

When we arrived at the house on the remaining piece of the original farm, my Uncle Domingo and his wife greeted us. The house was set back a ways from the road. The setting was beautiful: mountain views, green covered hills, cattle grazing, chickens foraging and tropical fruits and vegetation everywhere you looked.

During this visit, after we had been talking in the living area for a while, Uncle Domingo's wife and Lydia went into the bedroom and returned carrying a dust-covered paper bag. They called my father over, and all of them began talking very intensely in Spanish. A very dark look crossed my father's face. I sensed that the two women wanted to show me the contents of the bag. My father frowned at me and then at them, paused, and then with some anger and exasperation in his voice said, "Si!" (Yes!) My aunt put her hand into the dusty old bag and very carefully pulled out its contents. It was a faded wedding portrait of my mother and father!! It was the first time I had ever seen a picture of my mother. As I looked at every detail of this old 8x11 photo it dawned on me that my face bears a striking resemblance to my mother's face. Lois, Lydia and my aunt all wept tears of astonishment and joy. My father stood silently. I was stunned beyond response. I had found my face!!!

My aunt and uncle gave me the wedding picture to take home to copy. It felt as if they were giving me, literally and palpably, a missing piece of myself. I felt immeasurably grateful to them, especially to Lydia and to my aunt. I could see that these two women really knew how much it meant to me. It was a breakthrough moment.

There was something about that moment that began to tell me some of the mystery of my mother. Having a photo of her was a joy, and the joy brought with it a sense of wholeness I hadn't known before. For the first time I felt a satisfying connection to my mother.

But the wedding photo raised some haunting questions as well: where in Puerto Rico had she been born and raised? Where had she lived? Was her family still there and would I some day be able to find them and meet them? I wondered what she was like as a person and I wondered what had happened to her.

A Little More Information About My Mother

My attempts to raise these questions with my father yielded a little more information. He was tense, guarded and evasive. It was difficult and frustrating. Even so, he did tell me that my mother came from Las Piedras and that she had an uncle named Isaac and a sister named Dominga. Dominga had 3 children. He insisted that the whole family had moved to Washington, D.C. and he didn't know their addresses. He told me that my mother was orphaned at age 6 and then cared for by an Uncle Fernando and finally by her Uncle Isaac. He said Isaac came to New York after my birth, when my mother became ill, and insisted on taking her back to Puerto Rico where he was sure she'd get better. My father consented. My mother returned to Puerto Rico but did not get better. My father said she died in 1936 when I was about 6 months old.

All of this was sobering news, but I felt uneasy about it. It made no sense to me. I doubted that my aunt, her children and her uncle would all move to the States and then stay there. Something about the story didn't ring true. But why would my father be lying to me? After this incredible day of discovery and more questions, we all returned to my father's house exhausted.

Our Trip Comes To An End

After our visit to Aibonito our first three-week trip to Puerto Rico came to an end. We had had an amazing time. We'd experienced the joy of meeting my father's extended family. We'd enjoyed the culture and the food, and the beauty of the island. But our trip turned out to be much, much more than a simple vacation trip. My reconnection with my father was a powerful experience. Although he had been very gracious he had also been very evasive. I felt somewhat put-off and uneasy.

We'd also experienced the culture shock one might expect, and at times we were more than frustrated by our inability to speak Spanish. It would take us months to process all the experiences we had had. But for me, in particular, the unanswered questions about my mother were haunting. I was more determined than ever to continue my search for the truth about her life and death. I also wanted to know her family.

We arrived home to Chapel Hill and it was clear to me that I still had an incomplete family story. I was certain my father was withholding some very vital information about my mother, and it was clear that if I wanted to get the whole story I would have to get it without my father's help.

WE MOVE TO MICHIGAN: 1970

We returned to our life in Chapel Hill after our trip in the summer of '68, and I put my quest for my mother's family on the back burner. My professional life was intense, compelling and rewarding, and Lois and I were in the midst of raising three young children. Life was full. In 1969 I received an offer to join the faculty at the University of Michigan in Ann Arbor. It was one of those offers you don't turn down. In August of 1970 we moved to Michigan with great ambivalence. Lois, especially, was reluctant to leave our wonderful life in Chapel Hill and as it turned out, the children missed it too. Once in Michigan, we bought an older home on two acres. Lois always said the thing that sold us on it was the small stable on the back acre. We had promised 12 year old Kathleen she could have a horse. The house was OK, but it needed a lot of work. It became our "project", and we began to plan immediately for a family room addition. We got the kids situated in their schools and life in Ann Arbor was underway. By the time we finished the project we'd created a wonderful home in which to raise our children.

~ Answers At Last ~

PUERTO RICO TRIP #2: SUMMER 1971

During these years, after an additional round of letters between my father and me between the foster care agency and me, I remained convinced that I still didn't have the whole story about my mother. I especially realized this after I had written to my father proposing that the two of us go to Las Piedras to find my mother's family. He didn't respond to my letter nor did he ever mention it, which told me my hunches on this issue were right. So three years after my initial visit, in the summer of 1971, I decided to return to Puerto Rico to focus on finding my mother's family.

I knew it wouldn't be any kind of vacation so Lois and I decided that I should travel alone. I prepared by reviewing my high school Spanish. Once in Puerto Rico I thought of asking someone from my father's family who was bilingual to help me in this search, but when I thought about the complications of that and the divisiveness that might cause with my father, I decided against it. I would go alone.

I arrived there on August 21, 1971. I stayed with my father and Lydia. Relations with my father were still tense but I felt an increasing bond growing between Lydia and me. Although we could barely communicate I thought she was sympathetic to my cause. As I've mentioned, Lydia was an orphan and had grown up in difficult circumstances. I sensed that her gentle prodding behind the scenes might have prompted my father to share more information with me than he wanted to.

For whatever reason, soon after my arrival he gave me two more photos of my mother and told me she had been raised a Baptist. He pointed out that he had been raised a Catholic. He also told me he didn't know how to get to Las Piedras. I understood this to mean that he didn't know how to get there <u>psychologically</u>, because any map showed the road to Las Piedras! I decided not to disrupt the uneasy harmony that we had re-established and to respect his need for self-protection: I let the matter drop.

As we shared the first few evenings together our conversations ranged from family news to politics. He said he thought he saw through political ploys: he identified with the poor, was concerned about economics and was against the war in Viet Nam. He didn't believe Puerto Rico would ever become a state because of the inherent issues of language, poverty and color. He said that Puerto Ricans claim they are 80% white and 20% black, but he believes it's the reverse. (I didn't know where the island-Natives came in and I didn't ask.) He also wanted to talk about his eventual death. He said he was 69; he wanted Lydia to phone me when he died. He said he wanted to be buried at the U.S. National Cemetery in Puerto Rico, for veterans of U.S. wars.

I listened. I was just getting to know this man who was my father.

FINDING MY MOTHER'S FAMILY:
ANSWERS AND THE TRUTH AT LAST

On August 24 I borrowed my father's Volkswagen "Bug" and told him that I was going to visit a church in San Juan. My plan was to talk to someone at the seminary about my desire to find my mother's family in Las Piedras. The priest I talked with there suggested that I simply make a trip to Las Piedras. He said it was a small town and that I could probably easily find the family I was looking for. He knew there was a Baptist Church there if that's where I wanted to start.

So I set out for Las Piedras. The weather changed suddenly and I found myself in a tropical rainstorm. As I pulled to the side of the road, in the frame of mind that I was, I decided it was probably a monsoon! It was torrential and it lasted a long time, long enough to swamp the battery of the little car. It took the help of a kind Puerto Rican man to get me mobile again, but I finally did arrive in Las Piedras.

I decided to start my search at the small Baptist church. All I had was my mother's name in my head and her uncle's name written on a piece of paper. The minister was at the church and we managed to communicate: he in his broken English and I in my broken Spanish. He had recently moved to town and he didn't recognize the family name. He suggested that we go to the local hospital to see if there were birth and death records on file. There were files, but none for Margarita Colón-López.

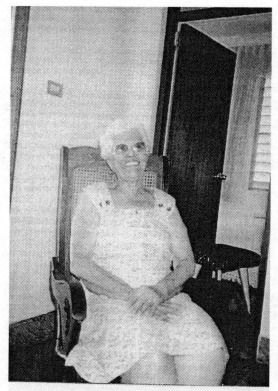

DOMINGA

Disappointed, we turned to leave when I happened to mention my great uncle Isaac López, who I assumed was deceased. The hospital clerk immediately recognized Isaac's name and directed us to his house. It was a bit out of town. We went there and I discovered that Isaac López was still living: he was 92! But he was in a deep coma, and his daughter Pura, who appeared to be in her 60's, was caring for him. She invited us into the house and asked if I'd like to see Isaac. As I stood looking at this old man I felt a great sense of gratitude to him and a deep connection to him. Not knowing how else to express these feelings I leaned over his bed and kissed him on the forehead. I stood back to look at him again, and then quietly left the room.

Pura, the minister and I began to talk. I mentioned Dominga, my mother's sister, and at the mention of her name Pura jumped up and became very excited.

Seeing me, learning my name, realizing I wanted to see Isaac and to find Dominga probably came all together in Pura's mind, and she realized who I was. She directed us back to Dominga's house, which was right across the street from the Baptist Church!

Once back in town the minister suggested I wait on the porch of his house, which was next to the church. He went across the street and knocked on Dominga's door. He seemed to be talking with her and then he brought her across the street to meet me. She was crying. When she saw me her hands flew to the sides of her face and she exclaimed, her voice full of emotion, "La cara, la cara!" ("The face, the face!") With tears of wonderment, joy and astonishment she embraced me. Dominga saw my mother's face in my face! I was moved and shaken by this encounter in a powerful and positive way. In Dominga's recognition of me, and in her hearty and precious embrace, I felt I had reconnected with my mother. I had found my face!

Dominga was a handsome woman with snow-white hair and looked to be in her sixties. I couldn't take my eyes off her. I wondered how much she looked like my mother.

Dominga and the minister began talking, and it seemed that I had indeed found my mother's sister, my aunt. I was stunned. After all the wondering and looking it had all come together so suddenly! It almost seemed too good to be true. I asked the minister to see whether there was any way she could prove our relationship. It seemed a little awkward at the moment, but I had to know for sure. She ran back home and returned with photos of her children Efrain, Evelyn and Harry and my mother and father's wedding photo!

She asked us to come in to her house and shaking with excitement and joy, she showed us another picture. It was me, with my dog Butch! Without a doubt, I had found my mother's family!!

Then the story began tumbling out. She said the whole family had been desperate to find out what had happened to Margarita's baby. Jaimie López, my father's friend, knew where I was. One time, she said, Jaimie, who was Isaac's son, arranged for her Uncle Isaac to visit me on Long Island, and Jaimie went along. Dominga's son Efrain, who was about my age, had gone with them. They reported back to the family that I was doing well in the foster home. They also took the photo of me with Butch and brought it back to Dominga.

Now I knew why I had felt such gratitude toward and connection to Isaac. Not only had he taken care of my mother when she was young, he had been instrumental in bringing news of me to her family. He also provided a connection to the family for me, ever so tenuous, but enough of a one that I was able to find them. Now I also knew who the mysterious people were who came to visit me so long ago at Mom Hauck's.

THE EVENING IN LAS PIEDRAS UNFOLDS

My Aunt Dominga wanted me to stay for supper and then go with her out to the farm to meet the rest of the family. But before I did anything more I decided to phone my father. I told him I was in Las Piedras and that I would be returning to his home late that night. Immediately I knew that he realized what I had done but he didn't ask me about it and I didn't tell him. I preferred a face to face conversation with him.

Eugenio and Isaura López, first cousins of Dominga and my mother now owned the farm. Isaura was Isaac's daughter and Jaimie López's sister. Eugenio's father was Don Fernando López, my mother's favorite uncle with whom she had lived when she was a child. My mother named me after him.

Once at the farm I met Eugenio and Isaura and their three adult children: Elisita 25, Eugenio 23 and Fernando 22, my second cousins! I was very warmly welcomed by all of them. Young Fernando could speak English, and he and I began to talk. I thought we even looked a bit alike.

He began to tell me what had happened to my mother. She was in the Rio Piedras Psychiatric Hospital near San Juan for 25 years. She died there, and was buried in Las Piedras. I was astounded.

Then I met Efrain, one of Dominga's two sons. Efrain and I had met once before: on Long Island when we were both boys and he had come to visit with Uncle Isaac.

And then: Jaimie López arrived! He beamed as he introduced himself, and said "Fernando, I'm glad to meet you. I've thought of you over the years, and I thought that when you became a man maybe someday you would come looking for your mother and her family and by God! you did!" He went on to say that my mother had been his favorite cousin, that he and my father were in the same army unit and became friends and that he had arranged for Margarita to live with the Falero's in NYC. He said that when he visited her there he brought my father along and that's how they met. He said they were secretly married in 1934 because the army didn't allow marriages without official permission from the "higher ups". Jaimie said he was in the Beth David Hospital waiting room with my father when I was born. Then he said, "After your birth your mother became mentally ill and was transferred to Bellevue Psychiatric Hospital and then to other mental hospitals in NYC. When she didn't recover, I made

FINDING MY FACE

the arrangements for her return to Puerto Rico to live with my father Isaac. She lived on his farm for nine months but still didn't get better. She would cry aloud and run away; they tried locking her in a small building and that didn't work either. When she was agitated she became very strong and only Eugenio could handle her. So reluctantly, he said, in 1937 they took her, by horseback, to the Rio Piedras Hospital where she was committed and stayed for the rest of her life, the next 25 years."

It was a lot of information. I was both relieved to know the truth and anguished to hear it. But there was more.

During the time she was in the hospital, Dominga, Efrain, Evelyn, Harry and Elisita regularly visited her. They were able to show her the photo of me and my dog so she could see that I was alright. Aunt Dominga told me with tears in her eyes that my mother always remembered me and always said my name, and at times she thought that Dominga's son Harry was me. Dominga also said that she thought if my mother had been able to see me she would snap out of it, and get better. I wasn't so sure of that, but I was convinced that it would have been good for both of us if we had not been separated at my birth.

The story went on. After my Mother returned to Puerto Rico my mother's family never heard from my father again. Jaimie reported that my father was afraid of my mother's "craziness". It may have been that my father's fear of my mother's illness made him determined to maintain the separation: between him and my mother and between my mother and me. Dominga had wanted to raise me and so had my grandmother, my father's mother. Gregorio would have none of it. He wanted me to be raised in the States so I could have a "better life".

His will prevailed at great cost to my mother and me. His decision left me cut-off from both sides of my family and the physical, emotional and spiritual losses that I experienced were significant formative factors in my life. His decision had a significant impact on my extended families as well.

Full of all this new information, I said good-bye and returned to Guaynabo expecting my father to be waiting up to see me. Not so! Lydia let me in at 11PM. My father was in bed. I wondered what would happen between us.

FERNANDO TELLS HIS FATHER THAT HE HAS FOUND HIS MOTHER'S FAMILY: 1971

The next morning I told him that I had been able to find my mother's family in Las Piedras. He was noncommittal. I told him further that he, Lydia and I had been invited to the farm in Las Piedras on Sunday for dinner. I assured him that the people I had met were wanting to "bury whatever hatchet needs to be buried".

He wanted to know who I'd met. I told him. His response was cool. He didn't seem to be pleased about this turn of events. I told him all was forgiven and they wanted to see him. His response was, "Yes, I did tell Isaac he couldn't see you anymore after that time he visited you. You told me you didn't want to see him anymore." I doubted that, but I let it go. In response to the invitation for Sunday he said neither "yes" nor "no".

TRIP TO THE RIO PIEDRAS PSYCHIATRIC HOSPITAL

After that difficult conversation with my father I went to the Rio Piedras hospital. I wanted to try to get the facts of my mother's life there. I was able to meet with the medical director and it was a most frustrating meeting. He was not forthcoming and was bordering on hostility. He sat behind his big imposing desk, opened my mother's file and asked me what I wanted to know.

Admission date? October 23, 1937

How long hospitalized? 24 years, one month and six days

Date of death? July 17, 1962 (I was 27 years old!!)

Cause of death? Aspiration of food

Diagnosis? Post-partum depression

and on and on…

The information was useful but I felt like I was talking to my father! This withholding process was making me angry and before I acted on it I thought I needed to say thank you and leave, which is what I did. Before I left the building I walked through the hospital a bit, trying to get a feel for what it must have been like for my mother. Grieving, I finally left.

MORE MATERNAL FAMILY CONNECTIONS

After I left the hospital I went to see my cousin Evelyn, Dominga's daughter, who lived in the Rio Piedras area. Like her mother, she greeted me with happy tears and hugs. She told me that she and Dominga visited my mother once a month through all the years my mother was hospitalized. I felt that now familiar gratitude once again. We had lunch together and then I returned to Guaynabo and my father's house.

When I returned my father said he wanted to talk with me. He said he'd been thinking all day and decided not to accept the invitation to the López family reunion on Sunday. He said he felt ashamed to face Don Isaac López. I tried to reassure him: Isaac is in a coma; he won't be able to recognize you; he can't even recognize his own adult children. But it was to no avail. He was convinced that the rest of the family remained mad at him for his refusal to let them have any contact with me. He said "that anger at me has spread through the whole family like a cloud". He was adamant. He did ask for Jaimie's address, and he said that "someday, in my own time, I'll go look him up and get him to talk to Isaac and the rest of the family, and see if we can't make this right". I suggested a phone call. He said "No. Person to person over a drink." He was immovable.

Much later my father did in fact make contact with my mother's family; with Jaimie and Dominga in particular. Jaimie told me later that Gregorio and Dominga had a sharp, emotional exchange. Although this meeting wasn't a happy one I was still relieved it had occurred. It helped Gregorio and Dominga deal with the truth, and that dealing helped toward healing a long-standing and deep family wound.

After my conversation with my father I went to see Dominga's other son Harry, my cousin, and his wife Sonia and their three children. Harry told me that he, like his sister Evelyn, used to visit my mother in the hospital. He said Dominga insisted on visiting my mother on a regular basis. The hospital was crowded and she was continually concerned about Margarita's well being. On his first visit to see my mother Harry said he was totally unnerved. The patients weren't drugged and they were "acting out all over the place". Dominga always felt some reassurance, because the woman who was the medical director at the time was a family friend, and so Dominga was relieved that there was someone on site looking out for Margarita.

As the years went by my mother became known as "Mother" around the hospital. She knew everyone. Throughout her illness when she seemed better Dominga would be elated, and then when she got worse again Dominga would be down. Harry said it was a real roller coaster for his mother. But she never gave up the hope that Margarita would eventually recover.

It was Harry and Evelyn who took responsibility for my mother's funeral. Her death had been upsetting to them. When they went to the hospital to take her body, it had not been prepared. They transported her to Las Piedras, and she was quickly buried. Only a few members of the immediate family attended her burial. With this news I felt my grief compounding.

Harry was angry at the way my father had handled the situation. He was angry with him for telling me my mother was dead and he was angry at the fact that he had kept me from the family. He said Dominga was angry with him too, and would remain so no matter what he did now. He was angry that he didn't even tell me the truth when I got older when it might have been possible for me to see my mother alive. Who knows, he said, maybe it would have made her worse or maybe it would have made her better, but at least you could have seen each other. Harry really helped me to get in touch with my own deep feelings about it all. I had been excusing and trying to understand my father's actions as a way of coping with the enormity of it all.

Harry was not of that mind and he was right. He thought there was no excuse for my father's behavior. He wanted to know if I had told my father what I had learned about the last 25 years of my mother's life. I said no, and as we talked I began to see that I had to have a frank conversation with my father. I was conflicted. Not talking with him would protect our relationship. But I now had a relationship with both sides of my family and I felt I was able to risk being totally honest with him about my grief and my anger. He was no longer the gatekeeper between my families and me. Harry impressed me: he was tough, aggressive, very intelligent, forthright and open but with sensitivity, feeling and compassion as well. Once again, I felt that sense of gratitude. I would talk with my father in the morning.

My Return Visit To The Psychiatric Hospital

Because my first visit to the Psychiatric Hospital was so frustrating, and I felt that I hadn't really obtained all the information that was contained in my mother's file, I decided to return to the hospital to see if I could find a way to have full access to her file. As I thought about it, I realized that the clerical staff started work at 8AM and the medical director started got to his office at 9AM. I arrived at the hospital at 8:00 and approached the record clerk, asking to see my mother's file. She remembered me from my previous visit, smiled, and said, "Of course." She got the record and asked me to sit at a location that I later realized was out of the line of vision of the medical director when he arrived. So I was able to spend a couple of hours reading my mother's complete record with the help of a Spanish/English dictionary. Finally, I had the full history and the full story about my mother's illness, hospitalization, treatment and death. I also found a 2x2-½ inch photo of her stapled to the file. This was a riveting photo: my mother as a psychiatric patient. As I looked at it I felt a wave of deep sorrow and sadness pass through my whole being. The more I looked at it the more I realized what her life must have been like in this hospital. It helped enormously to confront the tragedy and grief of her life. I decided I wanted to have a copy of this photo, but I feared that if I asked for it, I might not get it. So, taking a deep breath, I detached the photo from the file and put it in my briefcase.

Years later I enlarged the small photo so that I could really see and absorb it.

Now when I look at this enlarged photo I am able to see beyond the grief of her illness. I am able to see her strength, her intelligence and her tenacity as well.

During the 25 years my mother was hospitalized, my Aunt Dominga visited her about once a month. She always hoped and prayed my mother would get well. It was a sad journey for Dominga. She told me that each and every time she visited, my mother would ask, "Where's my Fernandito?" This touched me profoundly. In spite of the reality of our physical separation, she never forgot nor disconnected from me in her mind and heart. This repeated question told me of my mother's ongoing relationship with me that transcended our separation. This knowledge was an immeasurable comfort to me.

CONFRONTATION WITH MY FATHER

As I anticipated talking with my father my hope was that as we talked and I openly shared with him what I had discovered then he, too, might be truthful. I began by telling him that I realized that I now knew things that he didn't know about my mother's situation, and that I felt that he should know what I knew so that we might talk about it all. I told him what I knew. He became very angry and accused me of investigating him as though he were a "criminal". I acknowledged how he might feel that way but I also upheld my right to know what had happened.

Then he said, " I knew she came back to Puerto Rico. I knew she was crazy and I didn't want to tell you because I didn't know how your mind would take it. Such information might have affected you, and made you crazy too." I was too stunned to make an immediate response but finally said, "But when I was older, and a man......" He answered, "I was still afraid to tell you." And then, "Maybe I shouldn't have been."

It was a painful conversation but we stayed with it until we were finally able to talk truthfully with each other about these emotionally charged and difficult issues. His behavior and his secrecy finally made sense to me. He wanted to protect me. He had truly believed that it would be better for me to think that my mother was dead, and then he cut me off from her family to protect the lie. I was deeply touched by the dilemma he believed he was in.

As we talked, and he told me the truth as he saw it, somehow the shadow of the lie disappeared. I felt a wave of understanding, forgiveness and love for this man wash over me. My resentment and my anger dissipated. As we finished our conversation he said he was glad we talked, and we embraced each other in an act of forgiveness and reconciliation. I was enormously relieved. I felt so much better about him, and about us.

With all the pieces in hand I was sure the search had come to completion. The story from my mother's family, the truth from my father and the hospital record all converged. I had all the answers at last.

FAMILY REUNION AT MY
MATERNAL FAMILY'S FARM IN LAS PIEDRAS

The weekend came and I headed back to Las Piedras. Once I arrived there, Dominga, Efrain and Evelyn took me to the cemetery on the edge of town so that I could visit my mother's grave. It was old, with crumbling tombstones as well as some new ones; they were all jammed together in a small space. Some were newly white-washed and others were not but they were all surrounded by the light of a brilliantly sunny day. It was an emotional experience for all four of us as we stood before Margarita's grave. I realized that my aunt and cousins were weeping and then I realized that my own face was wet with tears. I had finally caught up with my mother. I felt profound resolution. The tie to my mother was no longer broken. Not even the reality of her death could change that. I felt the sacredness of the moment as I lay a bouquet of flowers on her grave. I gave God thanks for her life and for the life she had given me. I was at peace.

After leaving the cemetery we went on to the family farm which was set in the rolling hills outside Las Piedras. My second cousins Eugenio, Elisita and Fernando and their parents Eugenio and Isuara, who owned the farm, welcomed us. It was a joy to see how prosperous it was. There was pasture to graze 95 milking cows, and the pastures were bordered with lush tropical trees heavy with lemons, pineapple, avocado, bananas, oranges and plantains. There were calves, heifers, goats, pigs and 3000 chickens! Efrain showed me around and told me that they sold 2000 liters of milk every two days. I was amazed! We stopped by the old farmhouse. My mother had once lived there. I thought it had unparalleled charm. It was built with lumber from native trees. The main beams were constructed from tree trunks. The windows were open but could be closed with shutters. There were no screens. It was a charming, rustic, sturdy, very old farmhouse.

At the farm, Efrain had prepared a feast by slaughtering and roasting a young goat. Beer and wine flowed freely and all the guests took great pleasure in introducing me to their family food specialties: fried plantains, spicy rice and beans, chicken, corn, tomatoes, bread, home-made goat cheese, avocados prepared some wonderful way and an incredible mango flan baked by my Aunt Dominga. Other women in my mother's extended family prepared other dishes. They were all delicious! It was a great family feast!

Besides my Aunt Dominga about 30 other people came and stayed the day: first and second cousins, children, grandchildren, and other family and friends who had known my mother in her younger years. Throughout the day other people kept dropping by to meet me. I was overwhelmed with the joy of it all. As these people were introduced to me, one by one they would tell me a story about their experiences with my mother. In this way they were able to "give me my mother" in a way that transcended the harsh realities of her life and death. I was fortunate to be able to realize this while it was happening and I thought at once of the Biblical phrase "my cup runneth over". I knew this was surely one of those times. I was home at last.

As the celebration of my homecoming continued Dominga went into the house and brought out a large photograph. It was a group portrait of several families: Isaac

with his children and grandchildren and Dominga with her children and grandchildren. Everyone in the photo was someone I had met or had heard stories about that afternoon. Dominga gave me her radiant smile and gestured that she wanted me to have the photo. As she pressed it into my hand she said, "Tu familia" and then enveloped me in her arms once again, crying and laughing with joy. Dominga's hugs were powerful, and they transfused me with the fierceness and the strength of her love. She also gave me a photo of my mother as a young woman. What an incredible, unforgettable, heart-warming and heart-filling homecoming!!!

~ AFTER THE ANSWERS ~
AND THE TRUTH

RETURN TO MICHIGAN: 1971

I returned home to Ann Arbor to sift through all the facts and impressions and the memories of the three weeks just past. I tried to explain to Lois and the children the breadth and depth of what had happened, but it was hard to articulate. Once back at the office and absorbed in my professional life I had to set the immediacy of those memories aside. As I did I found they provided a strength within me that I cherished.

Lois and I took another quick break before the fall semester began to go to Michigan's Leelanaw Peninsula in the northwest corner of the state to look for property on Lake Michigan. We wanted to find a place to build a cabin so that the family would have a consistent get-away spot. Thanks to the help of our friend Leo Schmidt we found something a little south of the peninsula, took the leap and bought it. It was one of the best things we could have done. It became the anchor for family times then, and for years to come. What a summer '71 turned out to be.

The following autumn was packed, and there was little leisure for contemplation. Life was booming, it seemed to me, both at the university and on the home front. The kids grew like the proverbial weeds and our lives increasingly revolved around the opportunities and commitments that come with older children. We were reveling in their growth and development, alternately celebrating over their triumphs and successes and worrying over their potential problems. We were enjoying all their friends who came and went at our little country ce and all the action that accompanied them. Our new friendships in Ann Arbor took hold and flourished and it seemed to us that we were blessed with an abundance of just about everything. One of the greatest blessings was joining the First Presbyterian Church in Ann Arbor. It was a vital and engaged congregation and it became the foundation of our lives.

CONNIE BARRINGER-LÓPEZ: 1972

Before I left Puerto Rico Jaimie López had promised to put me in touch with his sister, Connie Barringer-López, who lived in Washington, D.C. Lois and I made a trip there to meet her and she turned out to be a treasure: a kindred spirit and a marvelous family resource. Connie and my mother Margarita were children together and cousins, both raised by Connie's father Isaac López.

As I came to know Connie I was aware of the fact that everyone seemed to be her friend. She related freely and warmly to family, friends and strangers alike and I noticed how generous and continuously helpful she was to everyone. She was the center of the communication network in the family: she was in contact with everyone and then informed everyone else what the others were thinking, feeling and doing! And she did it with caring and grace. She gave advice freely and had a great sense of humor. I came to regard her as one of the "angels" of my mother's extended family. Lois, the children and I had many good times with Connie: in D.C. , Ann Arbor and Puerto Rico.

When Connie retired she moved back to Puerto Rico and bought a condo on Luquillo Beach, which is on the eastern shore and about 15 miles from Las Piedras. Whenever we traveled to Puerto Rico after Connie moved there, she always invited us to stay with her. We spent many wonderful days and nights with her there, enjoying good food and conversation and the lovely tropical beach, complete with palm trees, rolling waves and crashing surf. We loved being with her and the time we had with her at Luquillo Beach.

Connie was very helpful to me, not only because she was a unique and wonderful person, but also because she was bilingual and could tune in to the complexities of my desire to know who I was, both racially and culturally. She understood the depth of importance I was experiencing in the newly established connections to my mother's family.

We spent hours talking about my mother: what her personality was like and how joyful and energetic she could be. She told me many details of my mother's early life and I never tired of listening. After she had known me a while she said, "You know Fernando, your personality is a lot like your mother's." I smiled and felt a great sense of satisfaction. Her sensitive remark made more tangible my sense of my mother in me.

Then one day she repeated the story I'd heard from Harry: about the delay at the time of my mother's death and her hurried burial. This time when I heard it I knew what I wanted to do: someday I would gather the family and have a proper memorial service for my mother.

Mom Hauck Dies: January 15, 1974

Mom Hauck and I had stayed in touch over the 20 years since I left home. At first we were in close touch and, as I've mentioned, she came to my graduations and we visited her a couple of times back East. As the years went on our contact was less frequent. I heard later from her granddaughter Carol that Mom wasn't in touch with her or her sister and brother much either after their mother Madeline died. Finally, Mom went to Florida to be the caretaker for an elderly woman who was blind. We found out later that she was older than the woman she was caring for which didn't much surprise us. That was Emma Hauck – up to the end.

I had known that shortly after I left "M" Street the two foster brothers who were still there went to other foster homes. Mom found work as a housekeeper and then as caretaker of a series of people who were either ill or disabled in some way. It was when arthritis became a problem for her that she took that commitment to care for people and moved to Florida.

I had been able to share with her my discoveries in Puerto Rico, how I had found my mother's family and the details of her life. I also was able to explain to her how I understood the reasons for my father's secrecy. She was eager to hear because she too had sensed that something was amiss with my father and she had often wondered what was going on with my families.

I heard from Carol, Mom's granddaughter, after Mom moved to Florida. She said that Mom wasn't responding to any efforts to reach her, so I decided I'd give it a try, and I phoned her. When Mom answered and said, "Who is this?" and I responded with, "Mom, it's Fernando" she slammed down the receiver! I was astonished, hurt and a little angry.

I formed a plan. I resolved to call her at the same time each week until she would talk to me. It took a while but it finally worked. It wasn't long before she began to chastise me if I didn't call at the exact moment she was expecting me on our particular phoning day! Week after week I tried to entice her to tell me what was wrong, why she had refused to talk to me and was refusing to talk to her grandchildren. I found out that she had decided that no one cared about her anymore. She began to soften and soon we were having long, wonderful conversations with each other.

One day I received a letter typed on a Braille typewriter by the woman Mom was caring for. Mom had had a heart attack and was in intensive care. She urged me to call the hospital, which I did. Mom was in critical condition.

Lois and I decided that I should leave for Florida immediately. When I arrived at the door of her intensive care room I was shaken. She was on a respirator and wired to more tubes than anyone could count. She was ashen. I went to her bedside and said to her: Hi, Mom. It's me, Fernando. She opened her eyes and I could tell she was shocked to see me. She smiled and started to cry, and then all the blood came rushing back to her face! I talked to her a little and then told her I'd be back often during the next several days.

Those visits are hung in time for me. We had some wonderful conversations reminiscing about our lives with each other. As these visits went on I decided to ask her a question that had puzzled me for years: I knew she had never warmed-up to Lois. So I said: Mom, there's something I need to ask you. Are you up for it? She looked at me suspiciously and then nodded. I continued then: I know you love me and I love you. I also know Lois loves me and I love her. But it seems strange to me: why don't the two of you love each other as well?

"Well," she said without a moment's hesitation and looking me straight in the eye, "I did all the work and she gets all the benefits." I was bowled over by her poignant and painfully honest response. I said, "I see, Mom. I think I get it now. But you should know that Lois really cares about you. It was she who did all the scurrying around to make sure I got down here to be with you as fast as I could." She looked at me skeptically and then said, "Oh yeah?" She was surprised and then pleased by this news. When I left to return home she asked to be remembered to Lois and the children. She and Lois subsequently talked on the phone a bit, and I knew that that relationship was a little better than it had been before. I was relieved, and so was Lois.

Before I left Mom told me what funeral arrangements she wanted when she died. I assured her that I would take care of them. We were able to embrace even with all the tubes. We said goodbye after four meaningful days of being with each other.

Not long after my visit Mom was returned home and slowly resumed her responsibilities with the woman she cared for. Shortly after that I received a phone call telling me that Mom Hauck had died of a heart attack while she was in the kitchen serving breakfast. The funeral home shipped her body back to New York as I had requested. She wanted to be buried in Rockville Center next to her daughter Madeline. Lois and I and the children attended her funeral and I was honored to talk about her life at the service. We accompanied her body to its final resting-place and as she was buried my thoughts were full of her 84 amazing years. What a difference her life had made! She was tough, and she could be difficult, but she had a "heart of gold". I knew that the good things in my life started at her knee and continued because of her commitment to me.

One of the blessings of the period of time around Mom's funeral was the reconnection with her grandchildren Carol, Arlene and Wesley. We hadn't seen each other for years. We had matured into quite a group, we decided, and it was a joy to be with them again. We promised to keep in touch. Some years later Arlene invited us to her daughter Stacey's wedding in Ohio, and once again, it was a delightful reunion.

Mom left a small inheritance for me, which I received in 1975. We were thinking about starting the construction of our cabin on the lake lot and this sum gave us the impetus to move ahead. How I wish Mom could know that her gift to me has multiplied at least 400 times. She would shake her head in disbelief and beam with satisfaction!

LIFE IN ANN ARBOR: 1975-1980

One of the joys of our new life in Ann Arbor was our participation in our church, First Presbyterian. In January of '75 I was ordained as an elder there. The privileges, responsibilities and challenges of that position, along with intense Biblical study, helped me to grow in faith and understanding. Lois was very involved in the church, too, and her faith was growing as well.

This growth was a gift on many levels, but we experienced it particularly in April of '76 when Lois' beloved mother died unexpectedly. Following her death we discovered that Lois' father was in the early stages of Alzheimer's. His decline over the next three years was painful for all of us and heartbreaking for Lois and her sisters. He died in June of '79. These two people had been anchors in our lives, a never failing source of love and encouragement and celebration of life. We would miss them keenly. In the midst of all this our two oldest children, Kathleen and Marty were leaving home and starting college. It was an intense time.

I had little time to visit Puerto Rico during this period of the 70's. Fortunately, some of the family there came to visit us. Harry Sanabria, Dominga's son and my cousin, and his family came. Connie came more than a few times; my father and Lydia came. It was exhilarating to welcome these members of my family into our home and into our lives. Harry's son, Harry Jr., who was our Matt's age, came for six weeks. He spoke English, but his parents wanted him to work with a tutor to hone his skills. He went to his tutor in the morning and then in the afternoon and evening he and Matt were free to do what they liked. They had fun, and Harry's language skills blossomed. When Harry returned to Puerto Rico Matt went with him and stayed with Harry's family for a while. I think it was a fun summer for both of them.

As the decade ended soberly with Dad Crump's death, we tried as best we could to set our sights on the future.

LOIS ATTENDS SEMINARY AND IS ORDAINED: 1980-1984

The future came soon enough as the future seems to do! In 1980 Lois entered the Clinical Pastoral Education Program at the University of Michigan Hospital. It was a year long and by the end she had decided she wanted to go to seminary. I wasn't too surprised and I was excited for her. Our pastor and her mentor, Bill Hillegonds, encouraged her and she had great support from family and friends. Finally she decided to apply, and she was accepted. In the Fall of '81 she began her three year seminary education, commuting each week to McCormick Theological Seminary in Hyde Park, in Chicago. She'd leave on Monday on the 8 AM Amtrack headed west and return on Thursday evening on the one headed east. It seemed to me (and to her) that she studied endlessly. Our life as we had known it was over!

She passed the ordination exams and graduated in June '84. Soon after her graduation she accepted a call as Associate Pastor to our own congregation, First Presbyterian in Ann Arbor where she served for 10 years. They were rich and demanding years and I watched with amazement as she embraced all the responsibilities thrust upon her. It was a stimulating, challenging, rewarding time for her and she loved it.

INVITATION TO A WEDDING IN THE FAMILY: PUERTO RICO 1982

In 1982, just before Lois assumed her duties at 1st Pres we made another trip to Puerto Rico. We had been invited to a wedding on my mother's side of the family. Dominga's granddaughter, Cuca, was the bride. My cousin Evelyn and her husband Miguel Hernandez were the happy parents. Miguel was President of the Senate of Puerto Rico at the time and Cuca's wedding was a gala occasion. 400 guests attended the wedding Mass which was celebrated in San Juan's oldest cathedral. The bride was resplendent in her gown; the handsome groom her counterpart in his tuxedo. It was an impressive, formal occasion complete with TV coverage.

The reception was elegant. All the members of my mother's extended family were there. Lois and I were honored to be seated at the head table with the bride and groom, their parents and other family members.

It was a truly joyous and memorable family event and a fascinating cultural event for us as well. We met family and friends from the city and the country: artisans, farmers, students, senators, businessmen and women, judges, shopkeepers, homemakers, and the former and current governors of Puerto Rico among them. The food and wine were superb. We dined and danced the night away. The band played a wide range of music, from the beautiful traditional romantic ballads of Puerto Rico to popular dance music. The music never stopped. It was a spectacular celebration and one we'll always remember.

THE MEMORIAL SERVICE
FOR MY MOTHER: PUERTO RICO 1983

We returned to two more busy years in Ann Arbor and when Spring Break approached in '83 I was ready for another trip to Puerto Rico. I had known my mother's family now for 12 years and I had been thinking a lot about the memorial service I wanted to have for my mother. I thought that this might be a good time to have it. It was scheduled for Thursday, March 10, 1983 at 4 PM in a small church on the outskirts of Las Piedras. Our senior pastor at 1st Pres, Bill Hillegonds, helped me plan the service. Connie and the local minister added their thoughts when I arrived in Puerto Rico. I had a copy of the complete service but it was in English. Miguel, Evelyn's husband, translated it into Spanish so copies could be made to pass out at the service.

March 10th turned out to be a beautiful sunny day. I had wondered if many members of the family would be able to attend because it was a weekday but it turned out not to be a problem. 33 people showed up and I was relieved and grateful. I shook my head in amazement and gratitude as Miguel arrived in his chauffeured limousine with motorcycle police escort. He was now President of the Senate of Puerto Rico. He had come to deliver the eulogy.

There were warm embraces all around and the service began. The pastor encouraged us to pray for Margarita and to release her into God's hands and into the fullness of life and health and to the glory of God. We celebrated the Lord's Supper and then the minister asked those who wished to speak to do so. Miguel spoke eloquently and movingly as did Elisita, Eugenio's daughter. Jaimie's son spoke as well. They spoke in Spanish but it was a powerful experience for me even so. I caught some of the meaning. Those who were mourning with me comforted me and I felt released from the burden of grief for my mother that I had carried for years. I felt that her life was duly honored. It was a time of grace.

Later Sonia, Harry's wife, and Connie told me what Miguel had said in his eulogy. He told once again of my search for my mother and of the family's knowledge of my mother's love for me even though we were never together. He said that I had always wanted her love, and wanted to return it, and that this service today was a way of doing just that. He also talked about her family loving me now in her stead, and as I return the family's love I am, in a way, able to love her also. He ended with: "And so now Margarita, who is present with us today in spirit, can rest in peace and Fernando, too, can rest in the joy and knowledge that all is well."

Miguel's words were healing words. They gave me a profound sense of resolution about my mother, Margarita López: her life, her death and her life eternal.

I was resolved and I was also exhausted. The next day I headed for the beach.

MY TRIP TO SPAIN: 1985

One thing that continued to intrigue me was the racial/ethnic make-up of Puerto Ricans. It seemed pretty clear to me from family information that they considered it to be Spanish, African and Island-Native, as they called the indigenous people.

So in the spring of '85 I decided to take a vacation in Spain and explore a bit of what that culture was like. It was the year of my 50th birthday and I thought a trip to Spain was a good way to mark it. I went around Spring Break, which included Holy Week. Lois was busy at the church so I went alone. If I'd felt odd-man-out in the blond blue-eyed culture of my childhood I certainly didn't feel that way in Spain! There were Colóns everywhere….it was a name like Smith is in the States. I traveled the back roads by bus and was able to rub elbows with all kinds of people.

I shopped in the shops and boutiques of Madrid and marveled at all the beautiful people: stunningly beautiful women and dashing men, some garbed in dress-capes over their business suits or evening wear. I had sophisticated Spanish cuisine and peasant fare. I had three stellar weeks in that culture. As Holy Week was observed I was able to see all the pageantry of the enormous religious floats quietly wending their way through the streets of Seville toward the Cathedral. They were supported and carried by scores of men hidden beneath their ornateness and lighted by thousands of candles. I was at the Cathedral at dawn on Easter morning when the huge doors of the Cathedral were thrown open and the float carrying the risen Christ emerged just as sunlight swathed the door.

It was a magnificent exposure to Spanish culture and its traditional Catholic legacy.

My 50th Birthday Celebration: 1985

Back home that summer Lois planned a celebration for my "big" birthday. It was a floating dinner party. 12 canoes were bound together in pairs, each set connected by a "table top". Linen, china, crystal, silver, candles in hurricane glasses and flowers adorned each table and

big luxurious pillows filled the boats for comfortable seating. The 7th set of boats had no table settings. Instead, much to my astonishment, a brass quartet took their place in folding chairs on that floating stage and we pushed off into the dusk to Handel's "WaterMusic". Once during that evening when the guests erupted with spontaneous

laughter and applause and I looked around at all those people I cared so much about I thought: I bet for sure it doesn't get any better than this! Thanks yet again to Lois and her ongoing fountain of love!

In the fall of that year I left the university where I had enjoyed so many interesting and productive years and went into full time private practice. Lois was totally involved at the church. I wouldn't have thought it possible for our lives to increase in intensity, but they did. It was a compelling and fulfilling time. There were no opportunities for trips to Puerto Rico.

Happy realities were unfolding though in our immediate family. Our daughter Kathleen married Dan Arrington in May of '87 and what an infusion of vitality, talent and warmth he brought to our family! In December of '89 Aisling Marie was born to Kathleen and Dan. Our first grandchild! How we fell in love with her!

My Father Dies: March 30, 1990

In March of 1990 my Aunt Luz's husband Luis called to tell me that my father was in a coma and near death in the VA Hospital in San Juan. I left immediately for Puerto Rico with our youngest son, 26 year old Matt. We arrived at the hospital to find that my father's status had not changed. His condition was critical.

The situation was sober indeed, and as I began to enter into it I found it to be an intense cultural experience as well as a sober one. The visits on the wards were communal gatherings of families and friends of all ages. Fellow patients knew all about one another's conditions and families. Matt and I learned that before my father lost consciousness he had told the other patients in the ward about me, my family and my career in the States. It was a little unnerving, but heartwarming too.

Matt, Lydia, my Aunt Luz and Uncle Luis, my cousin Nancy and I stayed at his bedside, and we appreciated the camaraderie. My father did not come out of the coma and died of heart failure a few days short of his 88th birthday.

The locus of our attention shifted to a massive urban funeral home where there seemed to be a dozen or more funerals being conducted simultaneously. My father's funeral was particularly meaningful to me because Matt was able to be with me and because both sides of my family came to give their last respects to Gregorio. I was moved by the fact that members of my mother's family came in spite of the history. They also attended his burial, which took place with full military honors in the Puerto Rican U.S. National Cemetery for veterans.

I hadn't developed a close relationship with my father in the years following our 1968 initial reunion. Even so, we had come to a mutual understanding and reconciliation of the difficult issues that had been between us. We'd left no unfinished business and I was grateful for it.

Aunt Dominga Dies: July 6, 1990

Three months after my father died my Aunt Dominga died, on July 6, 1990 at the age of 84. She had lived her life taking care of other people. I had had the privilege of knowing her for 19 years. I had developed a deep sense of love, affection and respect for her, and admiration for her loving, steadfast strength. What a significant difference she had made in the world.

~ 1994 – 1999 ~
WEDDINGS AND BIRT

1994, 1997 AND 1998
WERE BANNER YEARS FOR OUR IMMEDIA...

*Z*achary Richard Arrington, was born to Kathleen and Dan in April of '94, a healthy beautiful boy! Aisling now had a brother. We fell in love a second time with a grandchild, and our lives became increasingly involved with those two amazing children.

In May of '94, a month after Zak's birth, our Matt married Suzanne Keith at First Presbyterian Church in Ann Arbor. Matt and Suzanne had been in Ann Arbor for six months before their wedding, and we'd had a wonderful chance to get to know Suzanne. We were delighted and thrilled with our growing family.

Then in June of '97 Marty married Alexandra Davis in a lovely outdoor wedding in Bozeman, MT. Our two daughters-in-law brought zest and fun and creativity and all sorts of competencies into our lives. They also brought marvelous warmth, each in their own way.

In May of '98, Isabel Marlowe was born to Matt and Suzanne. I had to smile: what is it about these grandchildren? Once again it was love at first sight! Isabel was a marvel to behold! Getting to know her has been a source of ever-increasing joy and wonder.

ANOTHER FAMILY WEDDING
IN PUERTO RICO: 1999

My 13th trip to Puerto Rico was for a significant and gala event: the wedding of my cousin Nancy and Moncho Ramos. Nancy is my Aunt Luz and Uncle Luis' daughter

Nancy and Moncho's wedding turned out to be a country wedding. To say it was fabulous is an understatement! On this visit Lois, Kathleen, Dan, Aisling and Zak, and our sister and brother-in-law, Jean and Bill Carr accompanied me. What a time we had! The wedding was held at a beautiful facility in the mountains. We left the city in two cars, and began winding our way up into the mountains. The scenery was beautiful. We wound and wound and wound. Kathleen, no stranger to asking directions, kept us on

We did get lost several times in spite of it all, and each time Kathleen [would a]gain ask for directions. Complete strangers would drop what they were doing [to help] us find our way, often leading us for miles until we reached the next town or [turn i]n the road. This doesn't often happen in the States! We were having a grand [tim]e on this journey, except for the fact that I was getting tense because the time was [g]rowing short, I was sure we were going to be late and I didn't want to miss a minute of the festivities.

I shouldn't have been concerned. Even after we got there guests continued to arrive for over an hour. Moncho served wine and hors d'oeuvres, and we found out that they were waiting for a member of the wedding party. It was a perfect opportunity to absorb the beauty of the surroundings and the wonderful ambiance. Lydia was there, and some of my aunts and uncles. It was a joy to see them all.

Nancy and Moncho were married by the priest who was Nancy's friend from graduate school days at Clark University in Massachusetts where she'd recently completed her Ph.D. in geography. Even though we couldn't understand what was being said we could tell that the wedding service was full of life and joy. After the vows were exchanged Nancy, with her lovely voice, sang a love song to Moncho, and I doubt there was a person there who had a dry eye!

There wasn't a receiving line to greet the newly married couple. Instead, the guests rushed up to Nancy and Moncho hugging them, kissing them, laughing and crying and pummeling them with their joy. It was perfect! Dinner was served and the music began. The guests started dancing during dinner and on into the night. Everyone danced with everyone. Aisling and Zak were on the dance floor with the first of them, and I was delighted beyond words to see four-year-old Zak leading a congo-line of kids. Moncho's a musician, and his group provided the music. Lois and I couldn't believe it. It was a joyful, inclusive, exhilarating and exhausting celebration. We didn't want it to end.

It was gratifying to be part of the flow of some of the family events on both sides of my family in Puerto Rico. It was to the point where I'd seen a lot of these people many times, and life with them seemed to be more in the present than in the past. I looked forward to seeing them with happy anticipation and we were able to catch up where we left off. I was more familiar with the terrain. I was experiencing rootedness there, and I liked it.

REUNION WITH ARLENE AND CAROL: 1999

In the summer of '99 I had business in Washington. Arlene Amann, Mom Hauck's granddaughter, lived across the Potomac, in Virginia. We'd exchanged Christmas cards for years but I hadn't seen her since her daughter's wedding in Ohio. I thought this might be a good opportunity to reconnect so I gave her a call before I left Ann Arbor.

She seemed pleased to hear from me and invited Lois and me to stay with her, which we did. And did we have fun! Since she was older now I saw that her physical resemblance to Mom Hauck was striking. She was upbeat and outgoing and the stories about Mom Hauck started almost the minute we arrived. She'd tell some and I'd tell some. It was like opening a treasure box full of wonderful memories. She did actually bring out boxes of photos and we pored through them until the wee hours of the morning, talking and mostly laughing all the while. We had some serious moments too.

The next summer, Arlene and her sister Carol and Carol's husband Joe came to Michigan to visit us. Carol was so much like I remembered her: delightful, forthright and full of a marvelous sense of humor. I had known Joe when he and Carol were dating, and had had a good time with him at Arlene's daughter's wedding. It was good to be with him again; he was as much fun as he was in the '50's! Maybe this time together would be the first of many.

AUNT LUZ, UNCLE LUIS AND LYDIA VISIT ANN ARBOR: 2000

The following summer we welcomed Luz, Luis and Lydia to Ann Arbor. It was wonderful to have them with us. We took them around a bit, traveling to Indiana and Illinois to stay with Lois' sisters, and up to our place on Lake Michigan. I got the biggest kick out of watching Luz and Lydia pick up stones from the beach. They boarded their plane to return home with luggage many pounds heavier than when they arrived! We had had a wonderful three-week visit with them.

~ A MONTH IN PUERTO RICO ~
A FAMILY TRIP: 2001

A new Puerto Rico travel experience awaited us in February 2001. Our daughter, Kathleen, served as trip-planner, and what a trip she planned! At various times during our month there we traveled with Kathleen, Dan, Aisling and Zak; our sister and brother-in-law Jean and Bill Carr, and our nephew Jeff and his friend Clint.

Kathleen had us traveling from one end of the island to the other, east to west and top to bottom. We went from resort living on the ocean to staying in houses on stilts in the rainforest. We had separate cabanas on the northern coast for a few nights and time at Connie's former condo on the eastern coast. In the interior of the island, between Utudo and Lares, we went to the sacred grounds of the native Taino Indians: the Parque Ceremonial Indigena. It was a rich source of information on that racial stream of Puerto Rican heritage. Kathleen was fascinated, and Aisling ended up doing an impressive report on the Taino's when she returned to school. We made visits to various relatives on both sides of the family. Lucy and Albert, Aunt Luz's daughter and her husband, had a wonderful family party for us at their home near the northern coast. On the family farm, Elisa and Jose, Eugenio's daughter and her husband, hosted another happy family gathering for us. I was so glad that some of my U.S. family were getting to see these places that had become so important to me.

At the end of the trip Lois and I were there alone, and since all the activity was over I thought it would be a good time to see my mother's and father's birthplaces.

Aunt Luz and Uncle Luis took us to Aibonito where my father was born. We went into the nearby countryside to the place where my Uncle Domingo's son now lived. Luis took me about 20 feet from the house, into some tropical vegetation and pointed to some old posts stuck in the ground. They were the posts that held the house where my father was born. I looked around and in the distance, and could just about picture my father roaming these very hills as a boy.

The next day we went to the farm in Las Piedras to see if we could find the place where my mother was born. Elisita and Fernando, Eugenio's children now adults with grown children of their own, and Efrain, Dominga's son, met us there and took us by

four-wheel drive on a two track road way up into the hills at the back of the farm. We walked the last two hundred yards. Before us spread a panoramic view of the farm, the town of Las Piedras and the mountains in the distance. They pointed to a rectangular patch of grass that was darker than the rest. They said that was the footprint of the old house where my mother was born. Efrain said he could remember playing with Margarita in the surrounding fields and woods. I treasured this sense of my mother's life and where she came from. Elisa and Fernando smiled and said, "Fernando, this is an important thing to have done, visiting your mother's birthplace. You must write about it in the book you are writing about the family." I couldn't have agreed more.

~Aunt Luz And Uncle Luis ~
Celebrate Their 50th
Wedding Anniversary: 2002

In January of 2002 Lois and I returned to Puerto Rico to participate in the celebration for Luz and Luis' 50th wedding anniversary. My Aunt Luz and Uncle Luis have long been a part of my life, visiting me when I was in foster care with Mom Hauck and Dad Stewart. They were overjoyed to see me when I first came to Puerto Rico, in 1968. We've been in close contact with one another ever since that first visit over 30 years ago. Their welcome and involvement have been priceless to me. Each time we visit Puerto Rico and the family we feel more at home. When we arrived for this celebration, Nancy and Moncho picked us up at the airport and took us to dinner and to Old San Juan for an evening of nightlife

My Uncle Luis is a very lively, spry and handsome man who wears a mustache and always has a twinkle in his blue eyes, which sparkle with intelligence, mischief and humor. My Aunt Luz is a handsome, slender woman with a smashing smile and dark brown eyes that glow with warmth. She loves to dance! These two loaned us a car for the whole time we visited in 2001: a symbol of their unending generosity.

During one of our visits at Connie's condo, Luz, Luis, Nancy and Moncho came to spend the evening. We had a great Puerto Rican meal with chicken, rice and beans, plantains, flan and plenty of wine. After dinner Moncho played his guitar and Nancy and Aunt Luz sang wonderful old romantic ballads. Kathleen, Dan, Aisling and Zak were with us, and it gave us all a rich taste of Puerto Rican food, culture and music. Four year old Zak wore himself out dancing to the music.

My Aunt and Uncle's 50th wedding anniversary celebration was a wonderful family event. Again, what a celebration! A Mass was said celebrating their years of love and commitment; dinner and dancing followed. Family and friends came from all over the island to celebrate with them. The food was great, the wine flowed and music filled the tropical night. Moncho's band provided the music, and we couldn't hear enough of it. We had a wonderful time being with members of my father's family, including his wife Lydia.

Luis, Luz, Nancy and Moncho, Lucy and Albert, and Luis, Jr. always have been such marvelous hosts when we're in Puerto Rico. Their warmth and welcome remains with us even when we leave. Luis has this wonderful quip: "We've been saying goodbye so long I forgot we were leaving!" It gives a good clue: it's hard to leave.

THE SCULPTURE IN THE SQUARE
OF CONDADO, PUERTO RICO

During this '02 visit we stayed with Lucy and Albert, and enjoyed their wonderful hospitality. One evening my cousin, Luis Jr., asked me to come with him because he wanted to show me something he thought would interest me. He drove to Condado, and went to the town square. In the center of the square was a larger than life sculpture of three figures with their backs to one another, forming a circle. One figure was a Spanish conquistador, one was an African slave and the third was a Taino Indian. The work was dedicated to the contributions made to Puerto Rican history and culture by all three racial groups. I had been trying to figure out this heritage-mix for years, and here it was before our eyes in an art form! I couldn't quit looking at it. It was powerful, and an eloquent tribute to all three races.

Over the years I've collected some Puerto Rican art. I have a little collection that includes a piece of sculpture, two masks that are used to celebrate saints' days, some paintings and silk screens, and some ceramic Taino pieces. When I see these treasures in my home in Michigan I feel that I've been able to bring some pieces of my rich heritage home with me.

THE COMING TOGETHER OF BOTH OF MY FAMILIES
AT THE LAS PIEDRAS FARM: 2002

While we were at Lucy's I had been in touch with Elisita, who was now the matriarch on the farm and also an "angel" of my mother's family. Her generosity, and the generosity of her brothers Eugenio and Fernando and their wives, has always touched me. I contacted her this trip to see if I might bring Luz and Luis, Nancy and Moncho, Lucy and Albert and their two children out to the farm. She graciously agreed. It would be the first time both sides of my family had been together for simply a happy social event. It was a wonderful afternoon for me and everyone seemed to be having a good time. I greatly appreciated Elisita's and Jose's generous hospitality that made it possible. They served a delicious lunch in Elisita's wonderful country kitchen. Eugenio and his family, Fernando and his family, my cousins, Efrain and Cuca, and grandchildren were there,

The family farm in Las Piedras that is now owned and run by Elisita and her brothers, Eugenio and Fernando and their wives Awilda and Ada, has come to be a very special place to me. They have all created a solid, wholesome and satisfying life. They work hard and live well. Whenever I'm there, not surprisingly I feel close to them and to my mother as well. It was here that she used to live, and she roamed these hills when she was a child and a young adult. I draw upon and appreciate Elisita's, Eugenio's and Fernando's strength and positive attitude toward life. I feel immense gratitude that I've been able to find my way back to this family farm, and that I've been able to reconnect and reunite with this family. I feel a sense of gratitude in being reconnected to my father's family as well. It is these rich family connections that give me a sense of wholeness and strength.

As the afternoon unfolded I noticed that Elisita and Nancy seemed to establish a bond. And then at one point Lois realized they were having an intense, lengthy conversation. As the conversation ended they were crying, and they embraced each other. We wondered what had happened.

Later, Nancy told Lois that she couldn't stand visiting with my mother's family, accepting their wonderful food and laughing and talking as if nothing unusual had ever happened between these families. So, Nancy said, she spoke to Elisita about the sad circumstances of my childhood and about my grandmother's willingness to raise me, my father's stubbornness and the fact that he could be quite a difficult person. Elisita responded with the fact that their side of the family had wanted to raise me too, but they didn't know what had happened to me until Uncle Isaac visited me when I was in elementary school. Nancy said she wanted to apologize for her uncle, my father. Elisita understood. When I heard about this exchange I felt toward these women what was now that quite familiar sense of gratitude. It was another manifestation of the love of both families toward me.

Later, Nancy reflected with me about my efforts to reconnect with the family. She wanted me to know that since she was a child, my name had surfaced many times, "When we wondered how you were doing and what you looked like. I remembered seeing your picture with Mom when you were a teen. All they knew was that Fernando was a doctor and that you were married. Not much information but enough to make all of us very proud. I am very sure that if both my family and your mother's family knew that as a college student you were going through economic need, they all would have gathered some money to help. I still wonder…your father knew you were going to college and he never took the time to visit you and check how you were doing? God…of all of our family you were the first one to make it through college and later earning a doctoral degree!!! We wondered about your character. Finally you became a real person to us when Iris, who visited you when she was about ten years old and you were a teen, met you in New York City while you were attending a professional conference. She was a young woman then and she brought back a photo to the family to prove she had seen you. That happened a few years before your first visit to Puerto Rico in 1968. And because of all the visits you made to Puerto Rico to see us, it makes me think that even though your roots were cut and you grew disconnected from your family, you are indeed fortunate. You are deeply loved by two extended families in Puerto Rico and an extended family of your own which includes Lois' family. Your heart is linked to all of us and we are also fortunate to have received the gift of having in our family somebody so special, so brave, a real survivor."

Later, when I was talking with Elisita, she said, "You know Fernando, now you know you are loved by both sides of your family. Now we must all accept what has happened. Now we must go on." I've often thought of her wise words. The past is, indeed, over and gone. The future is always before us. And the present is very much with us. Now is the time for rejoicing.

So the long journey to understand my Puerto Rican heritage and to put together a coherent sense of who I am has been completed. It started with the few bits and pieces my father gave me when I was a child and has ended with the full richness and love that I now experience with both sides of my extended families. Each step of the way I've been enriched and blessed with a deeper sense of my Puerto Rican heritage: socially, racially and culturally.

I have found my face!

~ Epilogue ~

Photo by Bruce Gibb

It seems to me that every life is put together in bits and pieces: the family into which we're born, our innate personalities and gifts, and the experiences that we have. There are things that are thrust upon us and circumstances that overtake us as well as parts that we choose of our own volition. Our lives unfold from all these pieces and in that unfolding is our connection to the human family.

We all have stories to tell and it seems to me that they're all rich tapestries. I'm reminded of the beginning of the third chapter of the Book of Ecclesiastes.

For everything there is a season and a time for every matter under heaven:

A time to be born, and a time to die;

A time to plant, and a time to pluck up what is planted;

A time to kill, and a time to heal;

A time to break down, and a time to build up;

A time to weep, and a time to laugh;

A time to mourn, and a time to dance;

A time to throw away stones, and a time to gather stones together;

A time to embrace, and a time to refrain from embracing;

A time to seek, and a time to lose;

A time to keep, and a time to throw away;

A time to tear, and a time to sew;

A time to keep silence, and a time to speak;

A time to love, and a time to hate;

A time for war, and a time for peace.

God has made everything suitable for its time.

So many, many wonderful and good-hearted people have blessed the times of my life. The most important of these is my wife Lois, who married me 49 years ago when I had little more than enthusiasm. Her incredible steadfast love and support have helped me beyond measure to move through the seasons of my life with courage and faith. Each of our children also are gifts beyond measure or articulation, and they each in their own way have graced my life in ways they can never know. The opportunities to connect with my mother's and my father's families, and to remain connected to my foster family, and to be an integral part of Lois' family, have been key ingredients that have enabled seasons of my growth.

Everywhere I look in the life I have lived I see the reality of God's loving presence within the hearts of all the good people who loved, cared for, nurtured and challenged me.

I think of the time when I was three, when Mom Hauck took me to the Presbyterian Church and pointed me in the direction of the Sunday School. I think, too, of the way faith in God took root within me, and how that Presence has been a source of love, comfort, joy, healing, strength, determination, persistence and resilience. It has indeed been God's Grace that has seen me through and enabled me to accomplish whatever I have been able to accomplish. Without this reality within me, without Lois and our children, without our families and our friends and our faith community, my story would be very different.

Matthew and Suzanne

Marty and Alex

Dan   Matt   Marty
Kathleen   Suzanne   Alex

Matt   Dan   Marty
Suzanne   Kathleen   Alex

Isabel

Zak

Aisling

FINDING MY FACE

~ GENOGRAMS ~

Fernando's Father's Family
2003

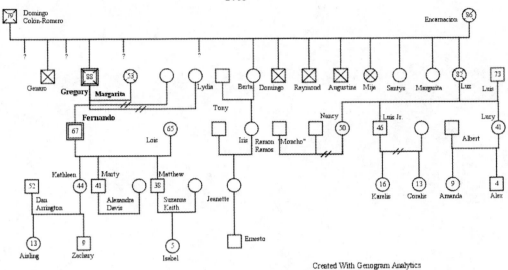

Created With Genogram Analytics

Fernando's Mother's Family
López, 2003

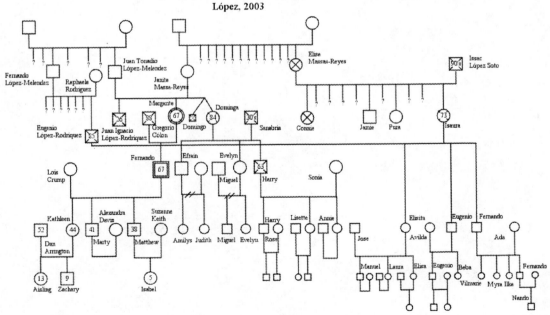

Created By Genogram Analytics

ISBN 1-41205307-2

9 781412 053075